"Most of us really want to p...
how to become people of prayer, people for whom it is as natural and consistent as breathing. Adriel Sanchez helps us in this quest, not by becoming a guru for prayer himself, but by showing us how Jesus comes alongside us in our feeble efforts to pray, helping us to rightly see who we're praying to, how we should approach him, and what we should talk with him about."

Nancy Guthrie, Bible teacher; author *of I'm Praying for You*

"No one wants to 'spam' God with prayer, but it happens, and it probably occurs more frequently than we'd like. It's why I love Adriel Sanchez's new book, *Praying with Jesus.* The author exposes tired, old habits that wheedle their way into our prayer life while affirming the delight we discover when conversing with the God of the universe. The book you hold in your hands will dismantle all pretenses in prayer so that your praise, confession, and petition are renewed and refreshed. The author offers the right mix of tender pastoral soul and a firm commitment to solid theology, and what he writes about Jesus's teaching on prayer will enrich your time with the One who cups his ear to hear your heart. I happily recommend this book."

Joni Eareckson Tada, Joni and Friends International Disability Center

"In *Praying with Jesus,* we encounter a profound exploration of the most important and well-known prayer in the Bible. Adriel makes it exceedingly accessible and illuminates its significance for our daily lives and our relationship with God. He offers refreshing wisdom, theological reflection, and practical insights on this timeless prayer."

Justin S. Holcomb, Professor of Theology and Apologetics, Reformed Theological Seminary; bishop of the Episcopal Diocese of Central Florida; author of more than twenty books

Praying with Jesus

GETTING TO THE HEART
OF THE LORD'S PRAYER

by Adriel Sanchez

New
Growth
Press

newgrowthpress.com

New Growth Press, Greensboro, NC 27401
newgrowthpress.com

Cover Design: Faceout Books, faceoutstudio.com
Interior Typesetting and E-book: Lisa Parnell, lparnellbookservices.com

ISBN: 978-1-64507-339-0 (Print)
ISBN: 978-1-64507-340-6 (E-book)

Library of Congress Cataloging-in-Publication Data
Names: Sanchez, Adriel, 1988– author.
Title: Praying with Jesus : getting to the heart of the Lord's prayer / by
    Adriel Sanchez.
Description: Greensboro, NC : New Growth Press, [2024] | Summary:
    "Adriel Sanchez explores the most famous prayer in history, the Lord's
    Prayer, and gets to the heart of each thing Jesus told his disciples to
    pray for"— Provided by publisher.
Identifiers: LCCN 2023044938 (print) | LCCN 2023044939 (ebook) |
    ISBN 9781645073390 (print) | ISBN 9781645073406 (ebook)
Subjects: LCSH: Lord's prayer. | Prayer—Christianity.
Classification: LCC BV230 .S265 2024 (print) | LCC BV230 (ebook) |
    DDC 226.9/—dc23/eng/20231206
LC record available at https://lccn.loc.gov/2023044938
LC ebook record available at https://lccn.loc.gov/2023044939

Printed in the United States of America

31 30 29 28 27 26 25 24   1 2 3 4 5

For my grandmother, Amelia Rodriguez.
Thank you for always reminding me to pray.

CONTENTS

Foreword

"I'm not feeling it," my kids say sometimes. When it comes to prayer, I've had those moments too. I *know* that God speaks to me through his Word and that I commune with him in prayer. I also *know* that communication is the heart of any relationship. It would be strange to pretend a loved one isn't actually living with you except when you're "feeling it." Another thing I *know* is that if I only prayed when I felt like it, I'd miss out on some of the best conversations. But it's easier sometimes to let the moment pass, like the morning jog or that long-overdue call to a close friend.

There's a difference, however, between knowing what's important, doing it, and feeling it. That's where this book on prayer can help.

I've benefited from meaty studies on the meaning of prayer. Meditation on God's character and all he has done to bring me into this communion stirs the embers, to be sure. But pondering the Lord's goodness isn't quite the same as actually talking to him.

I've also benefited from resources that focus on methods and regimens for daily prayer. But a danger to this approach is that I think more about checking the boxes and going on to the next thing. It's a shame when I turn privileged access to the throne of grace into a chore.

This book transcends theory and practical techniques. I cannot say you won't want to put this book down. In fact, it may lead you to put it down frequently—to pray. Drawing on rich biblical truths and meditations from counselors across the ages, *Praying with Jesus* is less a book *on* prayer than a book *of* prayer. Guided by Adriel Sanchez's pastoral insights, wisdom, and crisp prose that reads nearly like poetry, you will find yourself drawn by the triune God into his everlasting rest.

We are invited to come to the triune God just as we are, happy and heartbroken, restful and restless, in praise and lament, by ourselves and with the body of Christ. And, as Pastor Sanchez emphasizes, we come *with Jesus Christ*—not only as our mediator who prays for us but as our elder brother who prays with us. It is when we come in and with Christ, emboldened by the indwelling Holy Spirit, that we cry, "Abba, Father!"

> Since then we have a great high priest who has passed through the heavens, Jesus, the Son of God, let us hold fast our confession. For we do not have a high priest who is unable to sympathize with our weaknesses, but one who in every respect has been tempted as we are, yet without sin. Let us then with confidence draw near to the throne of grace, that we may receive mercy and find grace to help in time of need. (Hebrews 4:14–16)

Michael Horton
Professor of Systematic Theology and Apologetics,
Westminster Seminary California;
Founder and Editor-in-Chief, Sola Media

Introduction

Not too long ago, scientists discovered that they could store 215 petabytes of information in a single gram of DNA. For reference, that'd be like storing all the information *ever* recorded by humans in a space not much larger than your living room! Remarkably, something so small can contain more data than you could consume in a lifetime.

Think of the Lord's Prayer like DNA. As short as it is, it contains deep theological treasures that a lifetime of study couldn't exhaust. Born in the second century, the African theologian Tertullian said that in the Lord's Prayer one finds, "the whole record of Jesus's instruction, so that, without exaggeration, a summary of the whole gospel is to be found in this prayer."[1]

In the third century, the bishop Cyprian wrote,

> How great dearest brothers, are the mysteries of the Lord's prayer, how many, how magnificent, gathered together in a few words, yet abundant in spiritual power. There is nothing whatever with regard to our

pleading and our prayer omitted, nothing not con-
tained in this summary of heavenly doctrine.[2]

In less than one hundred words, the prayer Jesus taught
encapsulates not only the gospel, but the entirety of heavenly
doctrine! A wonderful example of the impact of this prayer
was the story told by Professor Kenneth Bailey. When he was
in Riga, Latvia, ministering after the fall of the Soviet Union,
he was struck by the fact that the seeds of faith were already
beginning to sprout so soon after the rock-hard soil of com-
munist totalitarianism had been tilled. Curious as to how this
could be, he asked a young woman where she had learned
about Jesus. She replied:

> At funerals we were allowed to recite the Lord's Prayer.
> As a young child I heard those strange words and
> had no idea who we were talking to, what the words
> meant, where they came from or why we were reciting
> them. When freedom came at last, I had the oppor-
> tunity to search for their meaning. When you are in
> total darkness, the tiniest point of light is very bright.
> For me the Lord's Prayer was that point of light. By
> the time I found its meaning I was a Christian.[3]

The Lord's Prayer is a beam of light piercing us through
with the good news of who God is and what he's done to
redeem his people. Yet despite this, many Christians have a
difficult time with prayer generally, and don't grasp the Lord's
Prayer specifically.

Prayer is a gift that eludes many of us. Like the sighting
of a rare animal, it's there for a moment, or even a season,
and then gone again to hibernate somewhere we can't seem to
reach it. We struggle to capture the habit of prayer with any
consistency.

Jesus tamed prayer when he gave us the Lord's Prayer. Here is a prayer that even children can say. I remember my mother leading me in the Lord's Prayer when I was just three or four years old. Once I had it memorized, I'd recite it nightly, thinking then that it was mostly a ward against nightmares. More than thirty years later, I've come to see that the Lord's Prayer *is* a safeguard against evil—but it's also much more. It's the gift of fellowship with the Holy Trinity, insight into God's purpose for your life, and a shovel for unearthing the treasures of grace. I hope to share this all with you in the pages ahead.

If you're already familiar with the Lord's Prayer, I trust this book will still benefit you. Even though it's the most well-known prayer in history, it's also the most misunderstood. Martin Luther observed, "Together with the name and Word of God, the Lord's Prayer is the greatest martyr on earth. For everyone tortures and abuses it; few joyfully use it correctly for comfort."[4] Luther recognized the difference between merely reciting the prayer and understanding the theological scaffolding upholding each petition. I want to take you beneath the surface of the words to understand the heart of the Lord's Prayer. As we uncover the rich and practical theology in each petition, there's less of a danger that the prayer will suffer another martyrdom at our hands.

In addition, it's my prayer that this book will strengthen your prayers, both in their consistency and in their content. I want to help you lay hold of what Jesus has captured for you: sweet communion with God through divine conversation. In his first sermon on the Lord's Prayer, fourth-century bishop Gregory of Nyssa said, "The effect of prayer is union with God."[5] I'd like you to experience something of this union as you read and put what you learn into practice.

This book is broken into two parts. In the first part, I'll define what prayer is and address some of the challenges we encounter when praying. I hope to give you some concrete ways to begin rediscovering the heart of prayer in your own life as we look at two warnings from Jesus, what the Bible says about how our bodies can aid us in prayer, and the ancient custom of daily morning and evening prayer. The second part of the book is an explanation of each petition in the Lord's Prayer. I've tried to draw out some deeper theological truths presupposed by the petitions, while also providing practical and pastoral insight. My hope is that this combination of theology and application will transform how you use the Lord's Prayer each day.

Each chapter ends with a prayer from the past. These prayers are borrowed from some of the godly voices that came before us, and they relate to the content of the chapter. They're also a reminder that you're a part of the universal communion of believers spanning space and time and that you're never praying alone (an idea I unpack in chapter 4). I encourage you to read these prayers slowly and then make them your own.

Finally, you'll note that I've provided some exercises to help you apply what you're reading, as well as some discussion questions for group interaction. Whether you read this book alone or with others interested in discovering the heart of prayer, it's my desire that the chapters ahead equip you to pray with—and like—Jesus.

Part One

General Teaching on Prayer

Chapter One

The Heart of Prayer

Let us not then make our prayer by the gesture of our body, not by the loudness of our voice, but by the earnestness of our mind: neither with noise and clamor and for display, so as even to disturb those that are near us, but with all modesty, and with contrition in the mind, and with inward tears . . . For not unto men art thou praying, but to God, who is everywhere present, who hears even before the voice, who knows the secrets of the mind. If thou so pray, great is the reward thou shalt receive.

—John Chrysostom, fourth-century
archbishop of Constantinople

An old monk tells the story of an experience he had while walking one morning. Alone in the woods, it seemed at first like the whole world slumbered. But for the white noise of a cold creek running nearby, there was silence. Without warning, a new sound pierced the creek and interrupted his meditations. It was a voice that the monk described as intoxicatingly celestial. He immediately began to look around, curious about its source. His eyes landed on a branch opposite him where a tiny bird had perched. It was a nightingale. He was struck by the beauty of the bird's song, how its throat puffed out and then exploded with praise. The monk couldn't help but cry as he heard the concert of the nightingale.

He asked himself, *Why is it doing this? Is it waiting for someone to praise it? Certainly not. No one is here. It didn't know that I would be passing by this way.* Struck by the fact that the nightingale raised such a melody for none but God, the monk exclaimed, "How marvelously you unceasingly carry on your duty, your prayer to God, O nightingale!"[1]

In prayer, we are to be like that nightingale. Prayer is the song of your heart to God. Sometimes it's an explosion of praise, and other times it's a trickling lamentation. In either case, the source of true prayer is the heart. Jesus made this clear when speaking about a group of people whose hearts were unchanged by God's love. "This people honors me with their lips, but their heart is far from me" (Matthew 15:8). God draws prayer out of his people like a person draws water from a well. Here, the man doesn't need water, but he wants it. God desires our prayers, and while they echo from our lips, prayer doesn't originate with the tongue. It reverberates from the deeper chambers of your heart, the wellspring of life (Proverbs 4:23). God wants to hear your heartfelt prayers.

This struck me recently when preaching through the book of Revelation. In chapter 8, John had a vision of Jesus, the Lamb of God, opening a scroll. When he opened the last seal of the scroll, there was "silence in heaven for about half an hour" (Revelation 8:1). Why the heavenly hush? Up until chapter 8, John described heaven as a place of thunderous noise. Imagine the voices of an innumerable multitude singing to God with full-throated vigor, "Amen! Blessing and glory and wisdom and thanksgiving and honor and power and might be to our God forever and ever! Amen" (Revelation 7:12). Then suddenly, they all stop.

As a minister without a church office, most of my work happens at coffee shops. Occasionally I'll try to get work done at home, but we have five children crammed into a three-bedroom house in urban San Diego. The love that fills our home is matched only by the decibels. Every so often I'll be at the house when an important phone call comes. Right before I answer the call, I hold up my cell and let out a big "Shhhhhh." Only when I've gotten the attention of my noisy cherubs and things have quieted down do I pick up the phone so I can hear the person on the other line. We ask for silence when we want to attune our ears to something, like a phone call or an important message. God is no different. He hushes the heavenly beings to listen closely to the prayers of his people.

Consider how Revelation 8 continues in verses 3–4:

> And another angel came and stood at the altar with a golden censer, and he was given much incense to offer with the prayers of all the saints on the golden altar before the throne, and the smoke of the incense, with the prayers of the saints, rose before God from the hand of the angel.

The silence of heaven makes way for the prayers of the saints. Now of course, God isn't hard of hearing. John's vision here is meant for us, to show us that our prayers are not drowned out by the noise around God. In his commentary on Revelation, theologian G. K. Beale notes that there was a tradition among some Jews that taught the angels in heaven would praise God at night, while Israel slept, but then remain silent during the day so that the prayers of the people could be heard by God.[2] In a symbolic way, Revelation communicates something similar. God is listening closely to our prayers. He's not distracted or busy with other things. He quiets heaven to hear the cries of his children on earth.

Jesus introduces the Lord's Prayer in Matthew's Gospel in the context of his Sermon on the Mount. He began his Sermon with what are known as the Beatitudes (Matthew 5:1–12), pronouncements of blessing by the King upon the meek and weak who long for God's grace. There, Jesus revealed to us that the kingdom we pray will come is given as a gift to those who are poor in spirit (Matthew 5:3). What does it mean to be poor in spirit? In part, it has to do with approaching God in faith. Greek scholar S. M. Baugh explains,

> As a key ingredient of faith, being poor in spirit conveys coming to Christ in want and need. The poor in spirit are embodied in blind beggars crying out by the roadside, "Lord, have mercy on us, Son of David!" (Matt 20:30; cf. Matt 9:27). It is the cry of a father who desperately kneels before the Lord and cries out, "My daughter has just died!" (Matt 9:18) or of a mother who has no other hope, "Have mercy on me, O Lord, Son of David; my daughter is severely oppressed by a demon . . . Lord, help me!" (Matt 15:22, 25) even though she is an outsider and unclean and shunned by Jesus' disciples (cf. Luke 7:11–15).[3]

You don't need to be super spiritual to pray; you just need to be poor in spirit. On the flip side, the more self-confident you are, the less you'll tend to truly pray. Prayer requires humility in that it's made from either a sense of need or gratitude. When you express your needs to God, you do so because you trust he's able to accomplish what you can't. When you give him thanks, it's because you recognize that he is the source of true beatitude, and not yourself.

The heart of prayer is a faith-filled approach to God that recognizes who he is. "Without faith" the author to the Hebrews wrote, "it is impossible to please him, for whoever would draw near to God must believe that he exists and that he rewards those who seek him" (Hebrews 11:6). God is the giver in prayer, and we come to him as needy, but loved children. How much faith do you need to pray? Jesus said less than a grain's worth would do the trick (Matthew 17:20). God doesn't despise the mustard seed faith of one who is poor in spirit. Jesus even ministered to a man whose faith was mingled with unbelief (Mark 9:24)! Faith is the vehicle that carries the imperfect prayers of an imperfect people into heaven, and Jesus is the one through whom those prayers gain a favorable hearing. Without faith and Jesus, however, it's a different story.

Two Types of Heart Disease in Prayer

Spiritual heart disease is the number one killer of an authentic prayer life. Before Jesus gives us the words of the Lord's Prayer, he warns us against two heart diseases that can infect anyone committed to developing a healthy habit of prayer. The first thing you need to watch out for is *hypocrisy*:

> "And when you pray, you must not be like the hypocrites. For they love to stand and pray in the synagogues and at the street corners, that they may be seen by others. Truly, I say to you, they have received their reward. But when you pray, go into your room and shut the door and pray to your Father who is in secret. And your Father who sees in secret will reward you." (Matthew 6:5–6)

The word that Jesus used in Matthew 6:5, *hypokritai*, was often used in the ancient world for play actors. If you've ever been to a live drama production, you know that the actors in the theater are only putting on a show for you. The best actors can almost convince you by their ability to embody a character. If they stick around after the production and you're able to meet them in person, you aren't talking to Hamlet or Macbeth, but Brian or Ted. One danger with prayer is that we can use it to put on a theatrical production for others. It becomes a mask we hide behind in order to pretend we're someone we aren't. The tragedy here is that if you only pray for other people to hear you, you're really trying to talk to them more than you're trying to speak with God. You're missing communion with God, which is the goal of prayer. God wants you to come to him and sincerely offer him the song of your heart.

Prayer should never be a performance for other people, but instead an offering to God. It's not your opportunity to display the depth of your theological knowledge or mastery of King James English. Corporate prayer is biblical (Acts 2:42), but prayer for performance's sake isn't. Jesus rebuked the hypocrites because they had reduced this means of union with God into a tool for their own self-exaltation. They were faking communion with God.

Think of a time in your life when you've "acted holy" to try and convince God, or others, that you were better than you are. My mind goes back to the first time I smoked pot in high school. The more stoned I became, the more the guilt of my Catholic upbringing plagued me. Convinced I needed to prove to God I was okay, I began to work my way through the Lord's Prayer while high. The twenty-second prayer seemed to last for hours, but my attempt gave me a bit of comfort. As strange as it sounds, we don't need a crowd to act like hypocrites. Sometimes we use spiritual things—like prayer—as a way of justifying ourselves before God. I was trying to use prayer for something it was never intended to be—a mask to cover deviant behavior. Tragically, some people never rise beyond abusing prayer in this way.

Consider many of the scribes, for example. They were a controversial group that had several run-ins with Jesus in the Gospels. The scribes were sort of like the Bible scholars of Christ's day. Alfred Edersheim noted how revered these Torah teachers were, "[The scribe] pushes to the front, the crowd respectfully giving way, and eagerly hanging on his utterances, as those of a recognised authority. . . . Each scribe outweighed all the common people, who must accordingly pay him every honour."[4] Beneath their pious frowns, many of the scribes in Jesus's day hid the deadly heart disease of hypocrisy. How difficult it must have been for them to hear Jesus's words: "This people honors me with their lips, but their heart is far from me" (Matthew 15:8). Jesus notices how they would offer up long prayers, not because they were eager to speak to God, but solely for pretense. For them it was just a show, and because of this, Jesus promises that they would receive greater condemnation (Mark 12:40).

Interestingly, the root of the Greek word for pretense there comes from the word "to shine." Prayer, Jesus says, is not your opportunity to shine before people. When our prayers become a way of trying to convince others, including God, that we're righteous, they've been infected with hypocrisy.

The second heart disease that is equally deadly to the life of prayer is *superstition*. Jesus went on in Matthew 6:7–8, "And when you pray, do not heap up empty phrases as the Gentiles do, for they think that they will be heard for their many words. Do not be like them, for your Father knows what you need before you ask him."

While the disease of hypocrisy is especially contagious in religious communities (like that of the scribes), this second sickness is prevalent among the pagans. We might refer to them today as "spiritual, but not religious." In Jesus's day, when the Gentiles prayed, they would heap up words and phrases thinking, *Maybe if I say this enough, or get the wording right, I'll unlock some divine power.*

It's been said that the phrase *hocus-pocus* can be traced back to the medieval mass. The priest, during the consecration of the bread and wine, would recite Jesus's words from the Last Supper in Latin, *"Hoc est corpus meum"* ("This is my body"). Unfamiliar with Latin, the average worshipper heard this as "hocus-pocus!" Certain that something miraculous was happening, the people came to believe the words carried some magical power. How easy it is for us to twist the things we don't understand! When the heart disease of superstition sets in, the words of institution in the Lord's Supper and the words of the Lord's Prayer become little more than incantations—things we recite while remaining in the dark. The words themselves are true, but when used as magic formulas to procure divine blessing, they mirror the pagan way of praying.

Handling holy things superstitiously is an age-old problem. In 1 Samuel 4, the Israelites carried the Ark of the Covenant into battle against the Philistines, treating it as a talisman of protection more than a means of experiencing God's presence. They were routed, and the ark was captured (1 Samuel 4:10–11). Similarly, the righteous King Hezekiah had to break in pieces the bronze serpent that Moses erected before the people because they had begun worshipping it (2 Kings 18:4). What had once been a great instrument of mercy (Numbers 21:4–9) had been turned into a staff of sorcery. In the New Testament, a group of Jewish exorcists once sought to invoke Jesus's name to cast out demons, even though they didn't have the Spirit of Christ living inside of them. The demon responded to their attempt by saying, "Who are you?" (Acts 19:15). Often, we want some magic object or formula to give us a sense of spiritual connection and blessing. However, prayer doesn't work because it's a magic formula. Prayer is a holy gift that must never be reduced to abracadabra or hocus-pocus.

You're familiar with spam emails: worthless information that fills your inbox; often someone trying to sell you something. Research has shown that nearly 50 percent of all emails that are sent are spam emails, billions and billions of emails *every day*. A very small percentage of people actually respond to spam emails and get tricked into spending money or giving away sensitive information. Nevertheless, spammers keep spamming because they know that eventually someone will bite. If they send enough emails to enough people, one of us is going to help the Nigerian prince or purchase the miraculous diet pills. The Gentile nations spammed heaven with their prayers. *If we just keep clicking "send," even though the words are empty, maybe God, or one of the gods, will bless us. Maybe we'll get a response.*

Don't spam God with your prayers. God knows what you need better than you do (Matthew 6:8). A simple and short prayer rooted in God's Word and will is more powerful than ten thousand empty phrases that seek to manipulate God. I should add, repetition in prayer isn't bad, but *vain repetition* is condemned by Jesus. One Greek word translates the two English words vain repetitions: *battalogeo.* The word is onomatopoeia (a word that mimics the sound it makes). It's like baby talk or babble. In Greek the word means to stammer, or to speak without thinking. You can't pray on autopilot and hope that the words you say are going to accomplish something magical without you having to think. That's superstition, not biblical prayer.

Ironically, both kinds of diseased prayer are ways we seek to manipulate. Hypocritical prayer seeks to manipulate others and cause them to believe that we're better than we actually are (sometimes we can even seek to deceive God by trying to demonstrate that we're okay, even though we aren't). Superstitious prayer seeks to manipulate God through the right words and repetition. Either way, in our attempt to manipulate, we're using the gift of prayer in a selfish and sinful way, which makes these kinds of prayer deadly.

Even mature Christians can contract spiritual heart disease. Praying for pretense and praying mindlessly can happen to you. The important thing is that you catch yourself when it happens and recognize that it's taking place. We rob ourselves of the true intimacy with God that prayer affords us when we pray in these ways that Jesus warned us against. The good news is that God extends you mercy when you fail. Our prayers this side of heaven will never be perfect, but they're sanctified by the blood of Jesus. In the words of the great Baptist preacher Charles Spurgeon, "The Christian will tell you that he weeps over his very tears; he feels that there is filth even in the best of desires; that he has to pray to God to forgive his prayers, for there is sin in the midst of his supplications, and that he has to sprinkle even his best offerings with the atoning blood."[5] The blood of Jesus Christ is the cure for diseased prayer. As we understand God's grace toward us in the gospel, we realize that we don't have to perform for others' sake or convince God we're something we aren't. We're free to let our hearts sing to the Lord without fear because we've been accepted in Christ.

A Prayer from the Past

Help us to set our hope on your name, Lord. You are the origin and source of all creation. You open the eyes of our hearts so we can know you. You alone abide highest in the lofty place. You are holy in the holy. You lay low the insolence of the proud, set the lowly on high, and bring down the lofty. You make rich and poor, give life and death. You alone are the benefactor of spirits and the God of all flesh. You look into the deepest places and see all our works. You help and relieve those who are in peril, and you are the savior of those in despair. You are the creator and overseer of every spirit. You multiply the nations and have chosen out all who love you through Jesus Christ your beloved Son, through whom you taught us, honored us, and set us apart. Amen.

—Clement, first-century bishop of Rome

Prayer Practices

1. Make a habit of reminding yourself before each time you pray that God is attentive to you. Try beginning your prayers this week by saying, "Dear God, thank you that through Christ, you're as eager to hear my cries as you are to listen to the voice of your beloved Son."
2. Reread Jesus's warnings in Matthew 6:5–8. Reflect on which of the two is most relevant for you and spend some time in prayer, confessing your own "heart disease" and receiving God's grace and help.

Questions for Discussion

1. If prayer is the "song of your heart" to God, what genre of music would you most associate with your current prayers? Are they full of grief and lamentation (the Blues), full of hope and joy (Jazz), or perhaps completely wordless (Classical)?
2. What is the relationship between faith and the heart of prayer?
3. What are some reasons you find it difficult to believe God hears your prayers? What did you think about the image of God "hushing heaven" in Revelation 8:1–4 to listen to his people's prayers?
4. Which of the two dangers Jesus warned against do you find yourself slipping into more: hypocritical or superstitious prayers?

Chapter Two

The Postures of Prayer

But on an ordinary day, who would entertain a doubt that he should prostrate himself before God, especially as we enter into daylight with the first of our prayers?

—Tertullian, second-century
Christian apologist in Africa

Your body is a spiritual instrument, not a spiritual liability. As a newer believer I didn't fully understand this. I assumed that the gospel mostly had to do with getting to heaven when I died. Heaven, as I imagined it, was a place of disembodied bliss, where we'd no longer be held back by the shackles of our physical limitations.

It's true that in heaven we won't have bodies. The time that spans the moment of our death until the final judgment and resurrection is what theologians call the *intermediate state.* This is a state of conscious existence in heaven, worshipping God together with the saints (every departed Christian) and angels (see Luke 23:43; 2 Corinthians 5:8; Philippians 1:23; Hebrews 12:23). As glorious as the intermediate state is, it isn't the ultimate glory that awaits us. Because Jesus rose from the dead, our bodies will also rise (1 Corinthians 15:20–21).

The implications of Jesus's resurrection for the physical world didn't begin to sink in for me until one afternoon at the park. Ironically, I was there sharing the gospel with strangers. I wanted to share the good news that *you too* could go to heaven when you die. Accompanied by a brother who had been a Christian longer than me, I'll never forget the question one man asked us: "What happens to my body after death?"

Thinking as I did at the time I wanted to say, "It doesn't matter because your spirit will be with Jesus!" Just as I was about to stick my foot in my mouth, my friend jumped in: "The Bible teaches that God is going to resurrect the bodies of every person who has ever lived. Some will be raised and judged for rejecting the gospel; others will be raised in glory." I nodded in agreement so as not to expose my ignorance! I had always assumed that the body was a sort of vestigial organ when it came to spirituality, something there, but unnecessary. I had missed the part of the gospel that promised the redemption of our bodies.

Christianity teaches that our bodies are the objects of God's redemptive love. Jesus's physical resurrection proclaims (among many other things) that God is for the body, and therefore our bodies must be for God. John Kleinig, a lecturer in theology and ordained minister writes, "Christian spirituality is embodied piety. We human beings are not just spirits, like the angels, nor animated bodies, like the animals, but are embodied spirits, or, if you will, spiritual bodies. We do not just have bodies; we are bodies."[1]

Since God created our bodies, they belong to him, but in a special way the bodies of believers have been purchased by Jesus. Paul said, "Or do you not know that your body is a temple of the Holy Spirit within you, whom you have from God? You are not your own, for you were bought with a price. So glorify God in your body" (1 Corinthians 6:19–20). Your body as a temple for the Holy Spirit is an instrument of praise *and* prayer. Prayer on earth isn't a disembodied spiritual exercise, but an offering up of the whole person to God (Romans 6:13; 12:1).

Why then do our bodies sometimes feel like more of a hindrance to prayer than a help? As soon as you say, "Dear Lord" the rest of your mind draws a blank. You've closed your eyes to pray, but your body thinks it's time for sleep. We're not alone in this struggle. Jesus's drowsy disciples had to be reminded that while the spirit was willing, the flesh was often weak (Matthew 26:41).

When our kids were younger, they used to blame their bodies when they didn't want to do something. We'd ask our son to clean up his toys and he'd respond by saying something like, "But my legs aren't working right now!" Or we'd tell our daughter to finish her dinner and she'd say, "My stomach says it doesn't want any more!" If you're a parent, maybe you've had this conversation too. Of course, my son's legs and daughter's stomach were working just fine; instead, it was a heart malfunction. They needed to bring their bodies into alignment with their hearts for the task at hand. We need to do the same thing when we pray.

The Postures of Prayer

The Bible suggests that our bodies have a part to play when we pray. In fact, throughout Scripture you get the sense that prayer is a *bodily* exercise! While I'd be willing to bet that most of us pray sitting down, people are rarely ever described in the Bible as being seated for prayer. From ancient times, prostration, kneeling, standing, and raising one's hands were the typical prayer "positions." Let's get into each one so that you can begin incorporating them into your times of prayer.

Prostration

Prostration is the posture of contrition over sin, best employed during times of repentance. When prostrate, our bodies cling to the dust of the earth, indicating an awareness of our mortality.

After the children of Israel had committed spiritual adultery with the golden calf, Moses said, "I lay prostrate before the LORD as before, forty days and forty nights. I neither ate bread nor drank water, because of all the sin that you had committed" (Deuteronomy 9:18). The Hebrew word *prostrate* basically means to fall, often used to describe someone who falls to their death (2 Samuel 21:22; 2 Kings 19:7; Amos 7:17). The psalmist said, "My strength is dried up like a potsherd, and my tongue sticks to my jaws; you lay me in the dust of death" (Psalm 22:15). And the psalmist also writes, "My soul clings to the dust; give me life according to your word!" (Psalm 119:25).

Throughout Scripture we see people prostrating themselves before God in confession: "While Ezra prayed and made confession, weeping and *casting himself down* before the house of God, a very great assembly of men, women, and children, gathered to him out of Israel, for the people wept bitterly" (Ezra 10:1).[2] In the book of Revelation, John described his vision of Jesus by saying, "When I saw him, I fell at his feet as though dead" (Revelation 1:17a; cf. Daniel 8:18).

Do you see the correlation? To be near the ground—cleaving to the dust—is to be near death. It's to enter a state of "deconstruction" if you will, returning (symbolically) to the place Adam was before God breathed life into him (Genesis 2:7). In repentance, we recognize that our sins aren't minor infractions, but violations of God's holy and perfect law. The sentence on sin is death (Genesis 2:17; cf. Romans 6:23), and true confession recognizes this. We lie prostrate before God as men and women deserving of death but raised up by Jesus

Christ. John continues in Revelation, "But he laid his right hand on me, saying, 'Fear not, I am the first and the last, and the living one. I died, and behold I am alive forevermore, and I have the keys of Death and Hades'" (1:17b–18).

We, those deserving death, come to the one who has the keys of death—the sinless Lamb of God who also lay prostrate in the dust of death for us. Matthew records, "And going a little farther *he fell on his face and prayed*, saying, 'My Father, if it be possible, let this cup pass from me; nevertheless, not as I will, but as you will'" (Matthew 26:39). Jesus, facing the cursed death sentence that rested on us, prostrated himself before the Father in the dust of our humanity to raise us up again.

Kneeling

Kneeling is a posture of gratitude, submission, and allegiance.

When King Solomon gave the prayer of dedication for the temple in 1 Kings 8, he praised God for his matchless love (8:23), but he also pleaded with God to continue hearing the people's prayers come sin or suffering (vv. 37–39). After this dedication, "he arose from before the altar of the LORD, *where he had knelt with hands outstretched toward heaven*" (v. 54). In Bible times it was customary to kneel before sovereigns to demonstrate submission and respect (Genesis 41:43). In 1 Kings 8, the all-wise king of Israel knelt before the higher sovereign: Yahweh, King of heaven and earth.

In Scripture, kneeling seems to be one of the most universal prayer positions. Daniel prayed three times a day on his knees, giving thanks to the Lord (Daniel 6:10). Stephen knelt in prayer for his enemies even as he was martyred (Acts 7:60). Peter knelt to pray for a sick girl named Tabitha (Acts 9:40). Paul frequently knelt to pray with the believers he ministered to (Acts 20:36; 21:5). When Paul prayed for the Ephesians, he said he did so with knees bent to the heavenly Father (Ephesians 3:14–16).

When we kneel in prayer, we're pledging allegiance to God with our bodies. The faithful remnant of Israelites who had not committed idolatry is described as being those who had not bent the knee to Baal (1 Kings 19:18). Bending the knee or bowing in worship is a sign of joyous submission for the believer (Psalm 95:6), and it's the acknowledgment that Jesus is the true king of our lives.

God promises that one day all creation will assume this position. "By myself I have sworn; from my mouth has gone out in righteousness a word that shall not return: 'To me every knee shall bow, every tongue shall swear allegiance'" (Isaiah 45:23). Paul applies this prophecy directly to King Jesus saying, "Therefore God has highly exalted him and bestowed on him the name that is above every name, so that at the name of Jesus every knee should bow, in heaven and on earth and under the earth, and every tongue confess that Jesus Christ is Lord, to the glory of God the Father" (Philippians 2:9–11). Jesus Christ is the King of kings and Lord of lords before whom we bow in prayer.

Standing

Standing is the posture of vigilance and being ready for battle.

As Christians, we are engaged in mortal combat against sin and Satan, and prayer is one of the ways we wage war. Paul said, "Put on the whole armor of God, that you may be able to *stand* against the schemes of the devil . . . take up the whole armor of God, that you may be able to *withstand* in the evil day, and having done all, to *stand* firm. *Stand* therefore, having fastened on the belt of truth" (Ephesians 6:11, 13–14).

While we bow before the true king in humble adoration, we *stand against* Satan and all his schemes, "Praying at all

times in the Spirit, with all prayer and supplication. To that
end keep alert with all perseverance, making supplication for
all the saints" (Ephesians 6:18). Jesus himself made this stand,
refusing to bow before the evil one (Luke 4:7–8). He taught
his disciples not to slouch in the face of temptation, but to
watch and pray lest they succumb to it (Matthew 26:41). We
too must stand attentive as watchmen and women ready to
heed the command of our Lord.

Among the Hebrews, standing was the primary posture
of prayer in worship. The early church followed this custom,
standing to pray when they gathered on Sundays. This reminds
us that gathering for church is itself a kind of warfare. The
gates of hell are plundered as God's kingdom is established
through the preaching of the Word, and the church militant
is given the rations of Christ's body and blood. We stand as
soldiers, ready to carry out his commands as we make our supplications known to God.

For the most part, when the Bible describes Jesus at the
right hand of the Father, it mentions that he is seated (Ephesians 1:20; Colossians 3:1; Hebrews 1:3). We know that Jesus
prays for us in heaven (Romans 8:34; Hebrews 7:25), and
there's evidence in Scripture that he stands to do so. When
one of Jesus's precious children, Stephen, was crying out to
him at the hour of his death, Stephen had a vision: "Behold,
I see the heavens opened, and the Son of Man standing at
the right hand of God" (Acts 7:56). This is the only place
in the Bible where Jesus is standing at the right hand of the
Father. Why the posture? Well, it's the posture of prayer and
attentiveness. In Stephen's darkest hour, while he was praying
for his enemies, Jesus was praying for him—attentive to his
suffering.

In those moments where you've wondered, *Is God attentive
to my suffering? Does he care?* Know that the Great King who
doesn't need to move a finger for anyone is roused to prayer by

the sufferings of his children. He sees to your needs. *Even Jesus stands to pray!*

Hands Outstretched

Hands outstretched in prayer is the posture of openness and offering.

Hands raised can accompany our prayers whether we're kneeling or standing. Paul said, "I desire then that in every place the men should pray, lifting holy hands without anger or quarreling" (1 Timothy 2:8). There's a vulnerability that comes with showing your palms to another person. You're saying, "I'm not armed; I come in peace!" Or perhaps you're communicating need, like the homeless man on the sidewalk who stretches his hand out as people walk by. When we raise our hands to the triune God, we're indicating that we've laid down the weapons of our rebellion and that our palms are open and ready to receive his divine grace.

A Warning Against "Going Through the Motions"

It's entirely possible that these postures can be entered into hypocritically. There are those who raise empty hands while carrying empty hearts. That was the case with Israel in Isaiah 1. God spoke to them, "When you spread out your hands, I will hide my eyes from you; even though you make many prayers, I will not listen; your hands are full of blood. Wash yourselves; make yourselves clean; remove the evil of your deeds from before my eyes; cease to do evil" (Isaiah 1:15–16). God sees the sin stains we try to cover with external shows of piety. Approaching him without dealing with those sins is dangerous. Before we raise our hands, we need to make sure they've been washed, and this is a cleansing only Jesus can provide.

Paul said that the body parts we once used for evil—including our hands—should now be presented to God as instruments for righteousness (Romans 6:13). The reason he gives for this is that God has washed us in Christ through holy baptism. Just a few verses earlier he wrote, "Do you not know that all of us who have been baptized into Christ Jesus were baptized into his death? We were buried therefore with him by baptism into death, in order that, just as Christ was raised from the dead by the glory of the Father, we too might walk in newness of life" (Romans 6:3–4). In baptism, by faith we were cleansed from all our uncleanness so that we might offer our-selves to God freely each day. We can come to God as washed sinners, no longer needing to pretend. We raise our hands and lift our hearts to God as living sacrifices. This also reminds us to use our hands for good!

St. John Chrysostom commented,

> What is the meaning of the extension of the hands?
> Since they minister to many wicked actions, such
> as beatings, murders, robberies, fraud, for that very
> reason we are bidden lift them up so that the ministry
> of prayer may prove a containment of these very vices
> and freedom from evil. The result will be that when-
> ever you are on the point of robbing or defrauding or
> striking somebody else, you may recall that you are
> soon to send these to God in the role of advocate and
> through them offer that spiritual sacrifice, and not
> shame them and render them mute by the ministry of
> evil behavior.[3]

"Do you kiss your mother with that mouth?" That's basi-cally what Chrysostom is saying, only a little differently. "Do you raise *those* hands to God?" When we lift our hands, we're reminded that those very hands are vessels for God's service. They're *his* hands, and every time we're tempted to use them sinfully, the lifting of the hands should remind us that our bodies have been purchased by the blood of Jesus. On the cross, Jesus stretched out his holy hands. His entire life was a prayer—an offering to God that culminated at the crucifixion. Through his offering, we can offer ourselves back to God in Christ—so lift up your hands!

Whenever you bow down, kneel, or raise your hands to the Lord, you're praying with your body. You're outwardly expressing what you also hope is the attitude of your heart. Prostrating our body recalls the death our sin deserves, kneeling the sovereignty of our Savior, standing the vigilance that is to accompany soldiers ready for battle, and raising hands remind us that we're in need of God's provision even as we offer him ourselves. There's no reason to be legalistic about these prayer postures, but we also shouldn't discount them. Sometimes in the spiritual life, the movement of our body precedes the movement of our heart.

When I was a kid, our family had an old car that frequently needed to be push-started. We'd be stranded at a gas station or grocery store, and my mom would enlist a group of bystanders to help push the car into gear as she'd crank the engine. With a little effort, we were back on the road again! When our hearts are cold, the postures of prayer can help to push-start our hearts into gear. Instead of viewing your body as a hindrance to the praying life, view it as a vital aid. Bring your body into the service of prayer.

Herman Witsius, a seventeenth-century Dutch theologian who wrote an entire theological manual on the Lord's Prayer, said, "Ordinary stated prayers, whether private, social, or public, require those postures which are fitted to excite and express humility, reverence, hope, ardor, and other affections of the mind."[4] St. Cyprian of Carthage wrote in the third century, "Let us call to mind that we are standing before the face of God. Both the posture of our body and the modulation of our voice should be pleasing to the divine eyes."[5] Your body belongs to God, and he calls you to offer it up to him whenever and wherever you pray!

A Prayer from the Past

We implore you, Father of the only-begotten, Lord of the universe, the one who has crafted all creatures, the maker of things that have been made. We stretch out clean hands, and we unfold our thoughts to you, Lord. Have compassion, spare, benefit, improve, and multiply us in virtue, faith, and knowledge. Visit us, O Lord. We display our own weaknesses to you. Have mercy and pity on us all. Lift up this people, and make us gentle and sober-minded. Cleanse us and set us apart to worship you rightly. Send your Holy Spirit into our minds and give us grace to learn the Scriptures and to properly interpret their meaning, that others may be encouraged through your only-begotten Jesus Christ in the Holy Spirit, through whom and to you be glory and strength both now and to all the ages of the ages, amen.

—SERAPION, FOURTH-CENTURY BISHOP
OF THMUIS IN EGYPT

Prayer Practices

1. Is there a prayer posture you have never used? Try that posture in prayer this week. What was helpful? Where did you struggle? Discuss the impact on your prayers with a family member or friend.

2. Are there unhealthy habits in your life that keep you from praying? Struggles such as excessive alcohol consumption, poor diet, or insufficient sleep can hinder the practice of prayer. Recognizing that your body is meant to be brought into alignment with the heart of prayer, consider what changes might be helpful in fostering an

improved prayer life. Discuss these challenges with a
friend who can encourage you in healthy next steps.

Questions for Discussion

1. How have you viewed your body in relation to your spiritual life? Why do you suppose we're tempted to think of
   it negatively, rather than as the object of God's love and
   an aid to prayer?
2. What is your typical prayer position? How do you hope
   to incorporate some of the biblical postures of prayer
   into your own life?
3. Can you think of biblical examples of people who went
   through the motions of piety without true faith? How do
   we guard against this, while not discounting the body?
4. Body image is something many people struggle with.
   How does Scripture shed light on the proper way of
   viewing our bodies?

Chapter Three

The Time to Pray

For we ought to think of God even more often than we draw our breath; and if the expression is permissible, we ought to do nothing else. Yea, I am one of those who entirely approve that Word which bids us meditate day and night, and tell at eventide and morning and noonday, and praise the Lord at every time . . .

—Gregory Nazianzus,
fourth-century bishop

A mysterious word at the center of the Lord's Prayer has stumped biblical scholars for centuries. It's the word *epiousios* in verse 11 of Matthew 6, which is translated *daily*. The trouble with the word is that no one can seem to trace where it came from. *Epiousios* was so uncommon in the ancient world that the third-century theologian Origen concluded that the Gospel writers had invented it!

Today, there are dozens of suggestions on how to translate this word, often drawing on the broader biblical story. Everything from the bread *necessary for existence*, to *heavenly* bread (an idea that can be traced to John 6:51), to the bread of God's *coming kingdom* (see Matthew 8:11; 26:29).[1] I'll get into the significance of this petition more in chapter 8. For now, let me say that I happen to like the word used by most English translations—*daily*. Like the children of Israel who gathered just enough manna for each day in the wilderness, we are to daily seek God for our needs.

This means that the petition for bread doesn't just tell us *what* we're to pray for, but *when* we're to pray. The rising sun brings with it new challenges that God wants you to depend on him to deal with. Each morning we ought to discipline ourselves to approach God in prayer.

Making Time to Pray

Somewhere along the way, many Christians started to equate disciplined prayer with rote or powerless prayer. We think, *How could something as intimate as prayer be scheduled?* I was shocked the first time I visited a church where someone prayed using a pad of paper. For me, the idea of prewritten prayers, or scheduled prayer, just seemed unspiritual. But it doesn't have to be. In fact, many of us wouldn't pray unless we forced ourselves to. From the earliest days, God's people have been taught that healthy prayer lives must be cultivated through hard work. It takes time, often *set-apart* time, to ensure that prayer is prioritized like Jesus modeled in his own life (see Mark 1:35; 6:46; Luke 5:16; 6:12; 9:28).

Setting apart time to pray is biblical. In Jesus's day, Jewish people were known to recite daily the words of Deuteronomy 6:4, "Hear, O Israel: The LORD our God, the LORD is one." This confession of faith in the one true God (offered when the worshipper rose from sleep and when they prepared for bed) was accompanied by prayers that magnified God by recognizing his provision and mighty works.[2] The pattern of individual morning and evening prayer reflected the corporate worship of the tabernacle, where sacrifices were offered to God each morning and evening (Exodus 29:38–46). Consider what the psalmist said, "Evening and morning and at noon I utter my complaint and moan, and he hears my voice" (Psalm 55:17). Or think about the example of Daniel: "He went to his house where he had windows in his upper chamber open toward Jerusalem. He got down on his knees three times a day and prayed and gave thanks before his God, as he had done previously" (Daniel 6:10).

It was this "prayer pattern" which Jesus's first disciples adopted. The early community of faith gathered in anticipation of Pentecost "with one accord devoting themselves to prayer" (Acts 1:14). This same phrase is used in Acts 2:42 to describe the rhythms of the early church: "[they] devoted themselves to the apostles' teaching and the fellowship, to the breaking of bread and the prayers." The apostle Paul encouraged this kind of prayer in the churches he ministered to (Romans 12:12; Colossians 4:2). One scholar observes, "The suggestion that this activity in a Christian context involves a different attitude and manner of prayer from those customary in contemporary Judaism, which had fixed hours and patterns of prayer has no real evidence to substantiate it . . . "[3] In other words, Jesus's disciples didn't abandon the pattern of disciplined prayer, but they embraced it!

Consider some examples from the early church that indicate there were common times set apart for prayer:

- In Acts 2:15 we're told that the disciples encountered the power of the Holy Spirit on Pentecost at the third hour of the day, the time for morning prayer (9 a.m.).
- In Acts 3:1 we read, "Now Peter and John were going up to the temple at the hour of prayer, the ninth hour." This would have coincided with the time of the evening sacrifice (3 p.m.). It's also when the angel appeared to Cornelius while he prayed (Acts 10:2–3).[4]
- In Acts 10:9, we're told that Peter went alone on a housetop at about the sixth hour to pray (12 p.m.).

These examples show us that the Spirit of God moves powerfully in and through disciplined prayer. As we read the New Testament, we can't help but notice that the followers of Jesus were serious about praying to God throughout the day, and they set apart time to do so. This is further confirmed by an admonition given in one of the earliest books on Christian living ever discovered, the *Didache*. The *Didache* is believed by many scholars to have been written around the same time as some of our New Testament books. In a brief section on prayer, it speaks of praying the Lord's Prayer three times a day (perhaps in line with the Jewish hours of prayer).[5] The biblical evidence in the Old and New Testaments, together with the practice of the early church, points to a pattern of disciplined prayer, often marked by prayer in the morning and in the evening (note also the repetition of "night and day" with reference to prayer in Luke 18:7; 1 Thessalonians 3:10; and 1 Timothy 5:5).

Do set-apart times of prayer contradict Paul's admonition to "pray without ceasing" (1 Thessalonians 5:17)? Not at all! They actually help us to carry out the command. In thinking through when people pray (including myself), I have noticed that we're often prompted by our feelings. When our hearts are stirred by a need, or we're filled with joy over some good news, then we pray. The problem with this is that our feelings are mercurial. If our feelings propel our prayer lives, then we are going to be inconsistent at praying, at best.

It would be like hitting the gym as often as you wake up with the rare urge to run on a treadmill. Many of us know what it's like to cross the threshold of the gym in desperation after the holidays, once our diets have been decimated and we feel the urgency to get back in shape. We can treat training in godliness just like we treat physical exercise. Undisciplined, we wait until our spiritual health is so bad that we must take action. Prayer that is only prompted by feelings will always result in praying less than we need to. This is why many of the wisest voices on prayer have encouraged seeing it as a discipline.

Witsius told his students, "Every person ought to select those hours which he finds to be most convenient for himself and his family."[6] There's nothing special about the times you choose. Everyone's schedule is different. The point is that we don't let our busyness get between us and our heavenly Father.

The French theologian John Calvin said,

> We are liable through the greater part of the day to the distracting influence of a variety of business, from the hurry of which, without laying some sort of bridle on our minds, we cannot escape. It is therefore, useful to have certain hours set apart for prayer, not that we should restrict ourselves to hours, but that we may be prevented from neglecting prayer, which ought to be viewed by us as of more importance than all the cares of life.[7]

Note the rationale. It's not that we're restricting ourselves to "times" of prayer in some legalistic manner, but that we're being careful to make sure we don't let the normal distractions of life keep us from prayer. A strong prayer life is something that is cultivated through consistency—but we must not confuse consistency with drudgery. Prayer isn't meant to be a chore, but a gift, given to us by God through his Son Jesus. If we get legalistic about times of prayer and treat them as a means of exalting ourselves, we're exhibiting the signs of infection with hypocrisy that I mentioned in chapter 1. C. S. Lewis has some wisdom for us on this:

> I don't think we ought to try to keep up our normal prayers when we are ill and over-tired. I would not say this to a beginner who still has the habit to form. But you are past that stage. One mustn't make the

Christian life into a punctilious system of law... [for]
two reasons (1) It raises scruples when we don't keep
the routine (2) It raises presumption when we do.
Nothing gives one a more spuriously good conscience
than keeping rules, even if there has been a total
absence of all real charity and faith.[8]

Building a consistent habit of prayer in your life is wonderful, but watch out that you don't turn your prayers into a
way of justifying yourself before God. If you do, then when
you fall short of praying your routine, you'll feel condemned,
and when you measure up, you'll feel conceited. Disciplined
prayer is nourished by the grace of God that has been given to
each of us. If our feelings or circumstances are what propel our
prayer life, the winds will come and go. But if our prayers are
set in motion by God's unchanging grace, then there's a steady
breeze we can draw from to motivate us each day. We wake up
each morning feeling different, but "The steadfast love of the
LORD never ceases; his mercies never come to an end; they are
new every morning; great is your faithfulness" (Lamentations
3:22–23).

Intimacy with God in prayer is a gift that has been secured
for us through grace. Paul writes, "When the fullness of time
had come, God sent forth his Son, born of woman, born
under the law, to redeem those who were under the law, so
that we might receive adoption as sons. And because you are
sons, God has sent the Spirit of his Son into our hearts, crying,
'Abba! Father!'" (Galatians 4:4–6). And in a parallel passage in
Romans he wrote, "For you did not receive the spirit of slavery
to fall back into fear, but you have received the Spirit of adoption as sons, by whom we cry, 'Abba! Father!'" (8:15).

You aren't a slave, forced to lay the bricks of prayer to meet
a quota of spirituality. You are a son or daughter of the Father
through Jesus Christ, given free access to God's inner courts.

Night and day his doors are open to you, and he invites you to come, lifting your hands to him because he's listening to you.

Let's look at three ways that I've been helped in prayer during those seasons when it felt like the well of my heart had run dry.

1. Using a prayer journal

There are many benefits to this, but I'll highlight just a couple. First, writing your prayers will help you keep your train of thought when praying. Have you ever sat down and tried to pray, only to discover halfway through the prayer that you forgot what you were talking to God about? It's happened to me! I've found that writing my prayers helps me to stay focused—to get from "Dear Lord" to "Amen!" without being distracted.

Second, your prayer journal becomes a monument to God's faithfulness. I love looking back on old "prayer entries" that I had completely forgotten about and being struck by the realization that God had answered a specific prayer I didn't even remember praying. We sometimes forget our prayers, but God doesn't. Your prayer journal can become a pillar of praise in the years to come.

2. Reading the prayers of others

The fact of the matter is that oftentimes you're going to show up to your prayer closet completely empty. You might have the time to pray, but you just don't have the words. Rather than only praying when you feel like you have something to say, I've found that using the written prayers of others can result in a very rich time of communion with God. *The Valley of Vision*[9] is a great little book of Puritan prayers that I know many have benefited from.

We also have an entire book of prayers in the Bible, which are known as the Psalms. The Psalms contain prayers for every season. Some are laments, for those times where God seems distant or you feel crushed by sin. Others are hymns of praise for when you can't contain your joy over God's blessings. Try praying through some of the Psalms in accordance with the season of life you're in. When you feel frustrated about the evil in the world, pray Psalm 10 or 73. When struggling with feelings of abandonment or isolation, pray Psalm 22. When humbled by sin, pray Psalm 51. When struggling to commit your trust to the Lord, pray Psalm 27, 63, or 131. When overwhelmed with God's goodness toward you, pray Psalm 8, 103, or 150. God has generously provided us with divinely inspired prayers for every occasion.

Of course, there's always the Lord's Prayer too! As we begin unpacking the theology behind each petition in the following chapters, you'll be better equipped to take your time praying through the Lord's Prayer each day.

3. Letting Scripture stir your heart

As we just discussed, Scripture is integral to praying consistently. Whether you're praying the Psalms or letting Bible reading stir up a heart of prayer, God's Word plays an important role in the praying life. When you feel like you don't have anything to say to God, let him speak first! I've had many cases of "prayer block" cured by reading Scripture. As I open and study it, I find myself responding to God's speech: confessing sin when I'm convicted, praising him when I'm awestruck, or even asking him for understanding when I'm confused. Take your Bible with you into the prayer closet so that when you find yourself with nothing to say, you can meditate on a few verses of Scripture and let the Word create the response of prayer in your heart.

I hope this chapter has been an encouragement for you to grow in the consistency of your prayers. May prayer become for you a daily habit that you dedicate time for, rather than an occasional response to life's circumstances. In the next chapter, we will explore the uniqueness of God as our Father in heaven. As we continue into the Lord's Prayer, I hope you will grow in praying more confidently (because you recognize *who* your Father is) and that the content of your prayers will be shaped by the teaching of Jesus and the Bible. May God continue to help us rediscover the beauty of Christian prayer.

A Prayer from the Past

As I rise from sleep, I thank you, Holy Trinity. Through your great goodness and patience you were not angry with me, a sinner who fails to act. You have not destroyed me in my sins, but have shown your love for humanity once again. When I was flat on my face in despair, you raised me to face the morning and to glorify your power. Now enlighten my mind's eye and open my mouth to study your word and understand your commands. Help me to do your will and sing to you in heartfelt adoration and praise, to your most holy name—Father, Son, and Holy Spirit, now and forever unto the ages of ages, amen.

—BASIL THE GREAT, FOURTH-CENTURY
BISHOP OF CAESAREA

Prayer Practices

1. Think about your daily routine and pick a couple of times throughout the day to schedule prayer—even if it's only for a few minutes! Set a reminder on your phone and find a quiet place where you can pray through the Lord's Prayer. In addition, think about one person you can pray for during those times of scheduled prayer, and reach out to them asking how you can pray on their behalf.

2. Get a prayer journal and set a goal of writing at least one prayer in it per week. Talk through the exercise with

someone in your church whom you believe can encourage you in prayer.

Questions for Discussion

1. As you look back on your life as a Christian, which disciplines have helped you to pray more consistently?
2. What do you think about the idea of scheduling prayer? Is there a realistic goal you can set for yourself in the days ahead to be more disciplined in praying?
3. Do you see prayer as a work to be done or a gift God has given to you? In what sense might it be a little of both, and what's the danger of seeing it solely as a work?

Part Two

Contemplating the Lord's Prayer

Chapter Four

Our Father in Heaven

Thus at the beginning of this prayer we are directed to
honor the Trinity as the creative cause of our coming
into existence. Further, we are also taught to speak to
ourselves of the grace of adoption, since we are worthy to call Father by grace the one who is our Creator
by nature.

—Maximus the Confessor, seventh-
century Christian monk

For God's people living in Old Testament times, no event
shaped their identity with relation to God more than the
Exodus. Their call to follow the Lord was to be especially moti-
vated by his redeeming love (Exodus 20:2). When God sent
Moses to Egypt to accomplish Israel's deliverance, he said to
him, "[Y]ou shall say to Pharaoh, 'Thus says the LORD, Israel
is my firstborn son, and I say to you, "Let my son go that he
may serve me"'" (Exodus 4:22–23). To address God as *Father*
meant for the Israelites that they were aware of their calling
to be rescued worshippers. God had brought them through
the Red Sea and claimed them for himself. Of Israel he said
"That's my son!"

To call God *Father* reveals something about your relationship with him too. He's your rescuer, the one who brought you out of the metaphorical Egypt of sin and death. Only those who have been adopted into the family are privileged with addressing God so intimately. When we realize that our adoption was the work of the Trinity—Father, Son, and Holy Spirit—we come to see that the beginning of the Lord's Prayer brings us into contact with each divine person. Put more simply, the words *Our Father* teach us about the rescuing love of the Holy Trinity.

Consider that for God to be called *Father* is to presuppose that he exists in relationship. God is a Father in two senses. First, he is the Father of his only-begotten Son, the Word. John said, "In the beginning was the Word, and the Word was with God, and the Word was God" (John 1:1). God never began to be the Father, but has eternally existed as One God, the Father (1 Corinthians 8:6). In this sense, he is *by nature* the Father of his eternal Son. Not nature in the way we think about human procreation and begetting, but with regard to the very being of God. Jesus and the Father enjoy an eternal, personal Father-Son relationship that is unique to them. Just as the Father never began to be the Father, the Word never began to be the Son. He is eternally begotten, outside of time, and beyond human comprehension.

God is our Father in a different sense than he is the Father of the Word. Jesus is the eternal Son of God by nature, and through his incarnation, life, death, and resurrection he has made all those who believe in him the sons and daughters of God *by grace* (John 1:12). The Father sent his Son and his Spirit to adopt us so that with Jesus, we too can call God *Father*. We join the ancient Israelites as those whose chains have been broken!

The relationship between adoption and freedom from slavery was picked up by Paul in the book of Romans, "For all who are led by the Spirit of God are sons of God. For you did not receive the spirit of slavery to fall back into fear, but you have received the Spirit of adoption as sons, by whom we cry, 'Abba! Father!'" (Romans 8:14–15). Just as God sent Moses to deliver the Israelites from slavery, the Father sent the Son to deliver us, making us his rescued worshippers. Of those who have received Jesus he says, "That's my son! That's my daughter!"

This means that every time you say *Our Father*, you should have two things at the forefront of your mind: First, you have the deep conviction that you are God's beloved son, or daughter, his very own rescued worshipper. Second, you cultivate an awareness of the benefits that belong to you as one adopted by grace.

The benefits of belonging

Growing up, my dad was a "cirquero," born into a family of circus performers. Together with his brothers, he owned a large circus that traveled throughout Mexico. Being the son of the ringmaster comes with its perks. As a child I had unlimited access to popcorn and soda at the concession stands. Later in life, when my wife and I were newly married, I impressed her one evening when I took her to a circus in San Diego and strategically mentioned to the person in the ticket booth that I was the son of Alejandro Vasquez of the *Gran Circo Hermanos Vasquez*. They let us in without paying! There are benefits to belonging!

What perks belong to you as a son or daughter of Yahweh? You've been given the family name, the gift of the Holy Spirit, and behind-the-scenes, unlimited access to God's throne of grace. If that wasn't enough, you are also the object of God's special compassion and protection, as well as an heir of everlasting life!

The family name was bestowed upon you when you received your *new birth* certificate in holy baptism. Since the whole Trinity is at work in our adoption process, we are washed with water in the name of the Father, and of the Son, and of the Holy Spirit (Matthew 28:19). This spiritual washing is another reminder of our deliverance from slavery. Like the Israelites who escaped Egypt by way of the Red Sea, we come through the waters of death and resurrection no longer under the dominion of sin, but instead under the dominion of the Savior (Romans 6:12–14).

When you believed, God gave you his promised Spirit as a gift (Acts 2:38). Think of this as a heavenly "first installment" with God himself pledging to see his purchase through and to lead you into the full inheritance that's waiting. Paul said, "In him you also, when you heard the word of truth, the gospel of your salvation, and believed in him, were sealed with the promised Holy Spirit, who is the guarantee of our inheritance until we acquire possession of it, to the praise of his glory" (Ephesians 1:13–14).

While we don't have our full heavenly inheritance now, we do have special access to heaven through Jesus. When the Word became flesh (John 1:14), he made himself one with humanity so that mankind, fallen in sin, might be reunited to a holy God. By faith and the gift of the Spirit, we are united to Jesus who is our heavenly representative and forerunner (Hebrews 6:20). One of our very own has entered heaven to stand on our behalf, and because of this we have behind-the-scenes access to God's throne of grace in prayer. We're insiders who can approach God with confidence (Hebrews 4:16).

The confidence of a beloved child

Biblical confidence isn't arrogance or presumption. The word used in Hebrews 4:16, *parresia*, looks more like the boldness of a child who is sure of her father's love. It was used in ancient politics to describe the freedom enjoyed by Greek citizens to speak openly. "The presupposition of *parresia* is that one should be a full citizen of a Greek *polis* [city-state]. At the height of Greek democracy the full citizen alone has the right to say anything publicly in the [assembly]."[1] Just as those with full Greek citizenship were given the freedom to engage in open political discourse, so too those who have been legally adopted by God as citizens of heaven enjoy the new birthright of open access to God, their Father. God looks at you, his child, with compassion (Psalm 103:13). He's like a Father eager to give you his best gifts (Matthew 7:9–11); not popcorn and soda but Christ, together with all the benefits Jesus secured for you on the cross. He distributes these gifts to you through the Holy Spirit, who makes us partakers with Jesus of the heavenly inheritance that awaits us, but which we've already begun to taste (Romans 8:17, cf. Hebrews 6:4).

As you approach God with childlike confidence, he wants you to know that your prayer-labors are not in vain. Think of prayer as a spiritual shovel, given to you by God to unearth all the treasures he has hidden for you in Christ (Colossians 2:3). The French Reformer John Calvin wisely said, "[T]o know God as the master and bestower of all good things, who invites us to request them of him, and still not to go to him and not to ask him—this would be of as little profit as for a man to neglect a treasure, buried and hidden in the earth, after it has been pointed out to him."[2] True prayer is never an exercise in futility, digging holes without purpose and coming up empty-handed. When we believe the lie that prayers are powerless, then rarely, if ever, do we commit to the labor of prayer. If, however, we recognize that prayer is one of the main ways we unearth the riches that are ours in Jesus, we're encouraged to approach God with confidence *and* expectation. Through prayer, your Father invites you to excavate the artifacts of his grace.

In Heaven

When my daughter Talitha was four, she was sitting by me on the couch as I scrolled through images on Google of outer space, marveling at the heavens declaring the glory of God, one sparkling nebula after another. As I kept scrolling, I couldn't help but notice her little brow was furrowed. Something was obviously wrong. Finally, she asked, "Where is Jesus?"

We had been telling our children that after Jesus's resurrection, he had ascended into heaven. Taking us at our word, she wondered why she couldn't see him floating by the Eagle Nebula. I explained to her what we meant by *heaven*—not outer space, as if NASA could discover the temple of the Holy Trinity. Heaven tells us of God's kingly rule and power—not the place of his confinement. God says, "Heaven is my throne, and the earth is my footstool" (Isaiah 66:1). When we pray to our Father in heaven, we're not putting God's address on our prayers. The words *in heaven* tell us that the God we pray to is all-powerful and transcendent. If *Our Father* speaks of God's closeness and the intimacy we have with him through adoption, *in heaven* reminds us of his greatness. Our compassionate Father isn't limited; he is infinite, eternal, and unchangeable!

Grasping this makes us think twice before flippantly approaching the throne of grace in prayer. Our manner of approaching someone often reveals what we believe about that person. I've heard it said that prayer is *just* "talking to God"— *as if God were just one of us!* Perhaps the reason we question his ability to answer our prayers is that we've come to believe this. Perhaps we've come to believe it because the manner of our prayers reinforces the lie.

We take God for granted when we address him as "the man upstairs" and border on replacing the intimacy we do have with an irreverence we shouldn't have. You *do* have intimacy with God, and such a kind that the angels covet. But the God with whom you intimately converse is also a consuming fire (Hebrews 12:29). Pastor Eugene Peterson illustrated this tension well with the following scenario:

> One of the indignities to which pastors are routinely subjected is to be approached, as a group of people are gathering for a meeting or a meal with the request, "Reverend, get things started for us with a little prayer, will ya?" It would be wonderful if we would counter by bellowing William McNamara's fantasized response: "I will not! There are no little prayers! Prayer enters the lion's den, brings us before the holy where it is uncertain whether we will come back alive or sane, for 'it is a fearful thing to fall into the hands of the living God.'"[3]

There's no such thing as small talk with God. Beware of approaching him with the kind of absent-minded chatter that is all too familiar in human interaction. Calvin said, "First, whoever engages in prayer should apply to it his faculties and efforts, and not, as commonly happens, be distracted by wandering thoughts. For nothing is more contrary to reverence for God than the levity that marks an excess of frivolity utterly devoid of awe."[4] The words *in heaven* provide a safeguard against the unholy indifference toward God that inspires aweless prayers.

God's heavenly transcendence also reminds us of his unlimited power. Back in 2002, a Denzel Washington movie called *John Q* came out. It's the gut-wrenching story of a dad whose nine-year-old son needs a heart transplant to live. The problem is that the family's insurance doesn't cover heart transplants. They seek alternative aid, but it's unavailable. Desperate, they sell everything they own of value and begin taking donations—but it isn't enough to pay for a new heart.

At times throughout the movie, it's difficult to watch Denzel's character. He plays the role of a father who would do anything for his son but is frustrated by a broken system and human limitations. He is a dad with unlimited love, but not unlimited resources.

You don't pray to a father like that. Ours is not a helpless and compassionate father, but the *heavenly* Father. He has infinite resources at his disposal to meet the needs of his people. Of course, he distributes those resources as he wills, but he isn't stingy, or cruel. He knows what you need before you even ask him (Matthew 6:8). Some people have a hard time praying with confidence because they doubt that God is their Father and that he cares about them deeply. Others lack confidence in prayer because while they've accepted that God is compassionate, they question his cosmic power. Our Father in heaven addresses the two lies that often keep us from praying: *God doesn't care about me*, and *God isn't big enough to address my problem*. God wants you to come to him knowing that *you are loved* and knowing that *he is able*.

The words *in heaven* also remind us that God is transcendent. This means that even though he reveals himself to us as a loving Father, it is beyond our ability to know him as he is in his essence. "For my thoughts are not your thoughts, neither are your ways my ways, declares the LORD. For as the heavens are higher than the earth, so are my ways higher than your ways and my thoughts than your thoughts" (Isaiah 55:8–9). When we pray to God in heaven, we're admitting that he's categorically stronger and wiser than we are. He is the infinite Creator, and we are his finite, but beloved creatures. It's this transcendent power that enables us to trust him even when things don't go our way. Prayer should lift our minds beyond the plane of the physical world and up to the place where angels live. In prayer, we approach the one who we know intimately, but who is wholly inscrutable: our Father in heaven.

Prayer Rope Team

Martin Luther said that when you pray, you should never think of yourself as praying alone. Instead, you come before God together with "all of Christendom, or all devout Christians, joining with you in a united prayer, which God cannot disregard."[5] This is true every time you utter the words *Our Father*.

Have you ever seen those pictures of mountaineers ascending a snow-covered peak in single file holding onto a rope? It's called a rope team. It makes a lot of sense that you'd want to be linked together like this while climbing an icy mountain. The rope provides a layer of safety for individual members of the group. If one person slips, the rest of the team can help stop him from taking the ultimate tumble.

The body of Christ is like an enormous rope team, making its way toward Zion's heavenly peak, and prayer is the rope that binds us together. Even in our "prayer closet," when we think we're praying alone, we aren't. Before we get to the first petition of the Lord's Prayer, it's helpful to note that the whole prayer is in the first-person plural: *Our* Father . . . give *us*, forgive *us*, lead *us*, etc. We're reminded that when we pray, we're bringing together the needs of the whole community of faith. I don't think we will know until we're in God's presence just how much we were sustained by the prayers of others—or how much our prayers helped to uphold them!

In his book *Losing Susan*, priest-scholar Victor Lee Austin describes his wife's battle with brain disease. Prior to her death, she reached a point in her sickness where prayer felt impossible. She understood the mechanics of prayer but had no appetite for it. He compared it to "having a five-star gourmet dinner delivered to your door but finding (or feeling) that your nose no longer smelled, and your tongue no longer tasted."[6]

What do you do in a situation like this? He continues,

[T]he prayers of a community can be strong enough
to carry along an individual who is, at a given time,
unable to pray. A sign of this is that in church each
of us doesn't have to be paying attention at every
moment throughout the entire liturgy. It seems to me
that God arranges it so that at any given time at least
one person is genuinely praying.[7]

Even when we experience prayer drought, we're carried
along by the prayers of God's people. Writing to the Philippians
from prison, Paul could say, "I know that *through your
prayers* and the help of the Spirit of Jesus Christ this will turn
out for my deliverance" (Philippians 1:19). This is great news,
but what if you're not on anyone's prayer list? In one sense,
we each benefit from the corporate prayers of the church. You
are included in the *our* of *Our Father*, roped in as the people
of God. In addition to this, we should also be comforted
by the fact that the captain of the rope team, Jesus Christ,
ever lives to make intercession for his people (Romans 8:34;
Hebrews 7:25).

You're never praying alone because Jesus is praying with
and for you. Above all else, the priestly ministry of Jesus
upholds you. When Jesus warned Peter about Satan's plan to
destroy him, he said, "Simon, Simon, behold, Satan demanded
to have you, that he might sift you like wheat, but I have prayed
for you that your faith may not fail. And when you have turned
again, strengthen your brothers" (Luke 22:31–32). Peter fell,
but the prayers and compassion of Jesus raised him to his feet
again. When you approach God's throne of grace, never envision
yourself alone. We come roped together with the whole
family of God, led by Jesus himself, and through Jesus we can
boldly say, "Our Father who is in heaven!"

A Prayer from the Past

I pray to you now, Almighty Father, with tears. I have called you unapproachable, incomprehensible, beyond measure. But I dared not say your Son was inferior to yourself. I have read that Christ is the radiance of your glory and the exact representation of your being (Hebrews 1:3). And I freely believe that you and your Son and the Holy Spirit are boundless, unmeasurable, inestimable, and indescribable. If I cannot measure you, Heavenly Father, can I without blasphemy discuss the secrets of your being? Can I say that Christ lacks anything when he himself said "All that belongs to the Father is mine" (John 16:15)? Scripture says an evil generation seeks a sign, but the only sign we receive is the sign of Jonah (Luke 11:29) . . . and the incarnation of Christ. Who has made me a judge between the Father and the Son, to divide between you and your Son, the glory of uncreated substance?

—AMBROSE, FOURTH-CENTURY BISHOP OF MILAN

Prayer Practices

1. Read Exodus 3:13–22 and Exodus 34:6–7. Write down some observations highlighting who God reveals himself to be for his people in those texts. Once you have a list, spend some time thanking God for the characteristics and attributes you see on display.

2. With the idea of a "prayer rope team" in mind, try to organize a prayer meeting with a group of friends from church (or see if your church leadership is interested in helping to get one started). Make a list of your church's specific needs, getting feedback from your pastor or other church leaders, and spend some time praying through those needs as a group.

Questions for Discussion

1. When you pray, do you find yourself focusing on one of the persons of the Trinity more than another? Which person, and why do you think this is? How do the words *Our Father* remind us of each of the three persons?

2. What aspect(s) of God as Father do you struggle to believe?

3. What are the implications of the Lord's Prayer being in the first-person plural (*our* Father)? How could the idea that we're linked together in prayer impact your own prayer life?

Chapter Five

Hallowed Be Thy Name

His name is said to be hallowed wherever He is named with awe and reverence. And this is what is now being done as long as the Gospel—by becoming known throughout the various nations—is making the name of God revered through the ministration of His Son.

—Augustine of Hippo

We come now to the first of six petitions in the Lord's Prayer. Before we start, I think it's important to answer one of the most common questions asked about prayer: Does it *actually* make any difference? You don't need to be an atheist to wonder this. After all, isn't God supposed to be omniscient? Jesus said God knows what we need before we do (Matthew 6:8). And if, as the apostle Paul said, God "works all things according to the counsel of his will" (Ephesians 1:11), what difference will our requests make in the grand scheme of things?

Some attempts to answer this question misunderstand how prayer works. Perhaps the most common is the idea that prayer bends God's will to our wants. Through prayer we're changing God's mind about the world and our circumstances in it. So we pray to move God to action, to generate in him something which otherwise would not be. The burden is on us, on our prayers, to create a change in God.

It's understandable that this might be our default understanding of prayer, but it isn't entirely accurate. Yes, our prayers do bring about change, but that change isn't foremost in God. Mysteriously, God uses your prayers to accomplish his sovereign and predetermined purposes, but the ultimate change is in us. This is what some of the greatest theologians in history have observed.

In addressing this very question, the medieval theologian Thomas Aquinas wrote, "We pray, not that we may change the Divine disposition, but that we may impetrate [ask] that which God has disposed to be fulfilled by our prayers, in other words *that by asking, men may deserve to receive what Almighty God from eternity has disposed to give.*" Hence, we pray "not in order to make know to Him our needs or desires, but that we ourselves may be reminded of the necessity of having recourse to God's help in these matters."[1]

Similarly, John Calvin said that God, "ordained [prayer] not so much for his own sake as for ours."[2] True prayer tethers us to God and refashions our hearts as they're conformed to his will. When you pray, the sovereign purposes of God are mysteriously brought to fruition. This means that prayer doesn't just bring about change within, it also changes the world around us. It can stop rain (James 5:17) and move mountains (Mark 11:23)! Prayer can melt the coldest hearts with repentance (Romans 10:1) and change even the direst circumstances (Acts 12:5). It's with this confidence that we begin, "Hallowed be thy name."

Make Your Name Holy

The word *hallowed* comes from the Greek verb to consecrate or make holy, *hagiadzo*. What does it look like for the Holy One to make his name holy through our prayers?

A friend of mine had a successful pest control business. When he was diagnosed with cancer, he didn't let it stop him from continuing to work. I called him over because our apartment complex was having a pest problem, and I thought it'd be a great chance to see how he was managing between chemotherapy and running a company. When he arrived, I was surprised to see him so full of joy. His cancer wasn't going away, and while he didn't minimize his pain and exhaustion, he clearly was not feeling sorry for himself. He said, "God has really used this cancer to chip away at the sin in my life." He smiled, with a look on his face that said, "Isn't that amazing!" He explained how his thinking had changed significantly since his diagnosis. He could see the sovereign and sanctifying hand of Jesus at work amid his suffering. Then he taught me an important lesson about hallowing the name of God. He said, "You know, we always talk about how we want to grow in Jesus. We want to be great for him. The older I get, I'm finding that I only get smaller, and God gets greater." His words immediately reminded me of what John the Baptist said as his ministry was giving way to Jesus's: "He must increase, but I must decrease" (John 3:30).

It struck me that this is precisely the kind of growth many of us don't want. We want to grow in Jesus in such a way that *we* are on display. The spotlight is in our strengths, as we become greater and greater for Christ. The trouble is that God isn't so much interested in hallowing our names, but his. My friend was weak and without strength, but in his weakness God's name was being hallowed.

The first petition of the Lord's Prayer is a request that God would demonstrate the holiness, greatness, and glory of his name in and through us to the whole world. God can't be more holy than he already is—so we aren't asking God to grow in himself, but in *us*. St. Augustine, the great Western theologian of the fifth century, preached the following to his congregation:

Why dost thou ask, that God's Name may be hallowed? It is holy. Why then askest thou for that which is already holy? And then when thou dost ask that His Name may be hallowed, dost thou not as it were pray to Him for Him, and not for thyself? No. Understand it aright, and it is for thine own self thou askest. For this thou askest, that what is always in itself holy, may be hallowed in thee.[3]

As with my friend, God may answer this prayer for you in ways you weren't expecting. Do you remember the conversation the apostle Paul had with God? Suffering from what he identified as a "thorn in his flesh," he pleaded with God in prayer to remove the cause of his suffering. Jesus responded to him by saying, "My grace is sufficient for you, for my power is made perfect in weakness" (2 Corinthians 12:9). God sometimes chooses to hallow his name not through our victories, but through our struggles. It may be the ongoing battle with sin that causes you to lean into his grace and rely on his Spirit, or the incurable cancer through which he exhibits the glory of his name in your grasp of resurrection hope. God is already making his name holy in you if you have the eyes to see it.

The Significance of God's Name

Names in the Bible are significant because they reveal something of the character or nature behind the one named. Jesus renamed two of his twelve apostles Boanerges, which means "Sons of Thunder" (Mark 3:17), to highlight something of their personalities. What is God's name, and what does it reveal about him?

When God called Moses to deliver his enslaved brothers and sisters, Moses wanted to make sure he could let the Israelites know who was behind the rescue mission. "If I come to the people of Israel and say to them, 'The God of your fathers has sent me to you,' and they ask me, 'What is his name?' what shall I say to them?" God responded in Exodus 3:14, 'I AM WHO I AM.' And he said, 'Say this to the people of Israel, "I AM has sent me to you."'" There at the burning bush God revealed himself to Moses as Yahweh, the LORD (v. 15). When you see in the Old Testament, the word LORD (all capitalized) instead of Lord, it is because the English text is distinguishing between the Hebrew divine name and the common word for Lord or master, which is *Adonai*.

The exact pronunciation of the divine name is lost on us. The ancients wouldn't vocalize it out of reverence, and in the Hebrew Bible, his name consists of four consonants (sometimes referred to as the tetragrammaton). While the proper pronunciation of God's name is unknown, the biblical focus was never on how the name sounded, but what it said or communicated. God's name is the revelation of who he is, especially in relation to his people. This revelation isn't limited to Exodus 3, but it encompasses the full range of God's actions in creation and redemption, spanning the whole Bible. Since Exodus 3 serves as a kind of "introduction" to the divine name, I'd like to camp there for a moment to better understand the hallowing of the Holy One.

The first thing to note is that the name of God in Exodus 3 is derived from the Hebrew verb "to be." We might say that when Moses asked God for his name, God responded by saying, "I am the one who is." Now think about that for a moment. Moses is about to go and challenge all the gods of Egypt, and each of those gods had a proper name by which the Egyptians worshipped it. Various pagan deities are named in the Old Testament, like Ba'al, Ashera, Molech, and Ashtaroth. As it is today, in Moses's time there were many "so-called gods," and so his response is even more striking. To the question, "What's your name?" God says to Moses, "I'm the one who actually has existence!"

Theologians have appealed to Exodus 3 to support an important but unfamiliar attribute of God. It's called divine aseity, from the Latin, *a se* meaning "from himselfness." *Aseity* means God has *self-existence*, making him completely independent (not reliant on anything outside of him). Practically speaking, this has significant implications when it comes to prayer. If God doesn't need anything outside of himself, then whatever he gives (through prayer) doesn't come with strings attached. He's generous and selfless in the gifts he bestows.

I remember as a kid watching the 1960s *Peter Pan* movie with Mary Martin. There's a scene in the movie where Tinkerbell gets poisoned and she's about ready to die. Because of her fate, I recall being on the verge of tears as a little boy. In the movie she assures Peter Pan that she can get better, but only if the little children believe in fairies. Then something strange (at least for films) occurs: Peter begins to talk directly to the watching audience as if he can see you through the television. He pleads with the audience to believe in fairies. If you believed (and I did), Peter invited you to clap loud enough so that Tinkerbell could hear you. My standing ovation revived the ailing fairy!

God isn't like Tinkerbell. He doesn't need our claps, our faith, or our prayers. He doesn't thrive on our worship, or our works. That might sound harsh, but it's actually really good news. Since God doesn't need us, we can be confident that he isn't a selfish lover. God didn't have a human-shaped hole in his heart that he needed to fill by making us. When mankind sinned against God, he didn't pursue us out of some deep insecurity. God made and saved you not because he needed something from you, but because he wanted you. Not to take something from you, but to give himself to you. God is the most generous giver there ever was. Realizing this helps us to better know that the God we approach in prayer in good (Matthew 7:11).

Paul praised the Lord saying, "'For who has known the mind of the Lord, or who has been his counselor? Or who has given a gift to him that he might be repaid?' For from him and through him and to him are all things. To him be the glory forever. Amen" (Romans 11:34–36). The God who needs nothing gives everything, not out of necessity, but out of the abundance of his goodness and love.

God's Holy Name Spread in Us and Through Us

Theologian Herman Witsius in his Sacred Dissertations on the Lord's Prayer highlighted three ways that God makes his name holy in his people.[4] The first way involves our growing in the true knowledge of God. When we apply our minds to know and acknowledge what he called the "Divine perfections," God's name is further hallowed in us. What are these Divine perfections? They're the ways God has manifested himself to us through his works and words recorded in Holy Scripture. This highlights how the true glorification of God (right worship and prayer) is inseparable from the true knowledge of God (right doctrine). We meditate upon Scripture so that we might know God not as we imagine him to be, but as he is in truth. Thus, the hallowing of God's name in us begins first and foremost with the personal knowledge of who he is.

This true knowledge of God should always lead to worship. Witsius says that we therefore must not stop at knowing the perfections of God but should celebrate them! This is the second way God's name is hallowed in us. "The knowledge of the Divine perfections must produce in us love, reverence, wonder, and adoration," he says.[5] A healthy hallowing of God's name in us looks like a growing awareness of God's perfections coupled with awe-filled worship. When we open the Bible for our "quiet time," with friends for a Bible study or seated in church on Sunday, we should be reminded of this petition and the means through which God often answers it. As the Holy

Spirit gives you a fuller understanding of who God is through Scripture, and you are led to marvel at his goodness in creating you, and his grace in redeeming you, God's name is being hallowed in real time.

Witsius added to knowing and celebrating God's perfections a third way by which we experience this petition: *when our whole lives are so regulated that our actions, as well as our words, tend to glorify God.* God hallows his name when we live for his glory instead of our own. This is a work accomplished solely by the Holy Spirit, who is sanctifying—making holy—the people of God day by day. When we pray *Hallowed be thy name*, we're asking God to sanctify us through true knowledge and right worship. "We sanctify the name of the Father in grace who is in heaven by mortifying earthly lust," wrote seventh-century theologian Maximus the Confessor.[6] Prior to Maximus, Gregory of Nyssa preached that in this petition we ask God to help us become godlier. He said the following:

> May I become through Thy help blameless, just and
> pious, may I abstain from every evil, speak the truth,
> and do justice. May I walk in the straight path,
> shining with temperance, adorned with incorruption,
> beautiful through wisdom and prudence. May I med-
> itate on the things that are above and despise what is
> earthly, showing forth the angelic way of life.[7]

This hallowing of God's name *in us* is also never meant to be just *for us*. Remember what Jesus said in his Sermon on the Mount? The good works God produces in us through sanctification are meant to lead to his glorification among the nations (Matthew 5:16). We're praying that God would diffuse the knowledge of himself throughout the world. Sometimes God's name is made known through judgment of sinners (Exodus 14:17–18; Leviticus 10:1–3; Ezekiel 28:21–22; Romans 9:22–24). Here God reveals himself as just, and insofar as this leads to a holy fear, God's name is hallowed. But more than anything else God wants his name to be hallowed *through the gospel*.

It's through Jesus that God's name is known and celebrated above all else, especially in the forgiving of our sins. Witsius called the forgiveness of sins found in Jesus "an incomparably bright exhibition of all the Divine perfections. There his love toward the human race, his wisdom, power, truth, justice, and particularly his holiness—shine with surpassing brightness."[8]

There is no place where God gets more glory than at the cross of Jesus Christ. On the cursed hill, the divine perfections radiated, piercing the dark clouds around Golgotha and proclaiming the hallowed name of God. It's there, in fact, that Jesus himself hallowed the name of his Father. In John 12:28, distressed about the hour of his crucifixion, Jesus prayed, "'Father, glorify your name.' Then a voice came down from heaven: 'I have glorified it, and I will glorify it again.'" Jesus explained to the crowd who was confused about what was taking place that he would soon be lifted up from the earth in order to draw the nations to himself (John 12:32). God's name is maximally glorified through the lifting up of Jesus on the cross in order to draw people from every nation into his kingdom—a kingdom which is here, and yet still coming.

A Prayer from the Past

> *Great art thou, O Lord, and greatly to be praised; great is thy power, and infinite is thy wisdom." And man desires to praise thee, for he is a part of thy creation; he bears his mortality about him and carries the evidence of his sin and the proof that thou dost resist the proud. Still he desires to praise thee, this man who is only a small part of thy creation. Thou hast prompted him, that he should delight to praise thee, for thou hast made us for thyself and restless is our heart until it comes to rest in thee.*

*Grant me, O Lord, to know and understand whether
first to invoke thee or to praise thee; whether first to know
thee or call upon thee. [. . .] I will seek thee, O Lord,
and call upon thee. I call upon thee, O Lord, in my faith
which thou hast given me, which thou hast inspired in
me through the humanity of thy Son, and through the
ministry of thy preacher.*

—AUGUSTINE OF HIPPO

Prayer Practices

1. Read Ezekiel 36:22–36. In what ways does this passage
   show that God's name is hallowed in his people and
   throughout the world? Spend some time listing specific
   ways God's name can be hallowed in and around you
   and pray for those things every time you say the Lord's
   Prayer.
2. Read Psalms 97, 102, 103 and 145 this week. As you
   do, make a list of the "divine perfections" you find in
   them. Once you have your list, prayerfully move from
   meditating on these characteristics to giving thanks to
   the Lord for how you see his divine perfections at work
   in your life.

Questions for Discussion

1. Can you think of a time in your life when God made his
   name great *through your weakness?*
2. In what ways are you tempted to treat God as if he
   depends on us? How do you see this manifest in your
   prayer life?
3. In what ways does our view of God influence our view
   of prayer?

Chapter Six

Thy Kingdom Come

So let your Kingdom come, Lord, all the more speedily,
the desire of Christians, the confounding of the gentiles, the joy of angels, for which we are afflicted, for
which we pray all the more fervently.

—Tertullian

The first *real* camping trip our family ever took was to southern Utah. At the top of our list of things to do was explore
Bryce Canyon National Park. I had always wanted to see the
towering hoodoos and red rock walls. If you don't know what a
hoodoo is, it's a rock formation that looks like it was created by
a giant who came and balanced boulders on top of each other.
The rock towers remind me of the sandcastles we used to make
as kids at the beach. Taking a fistful of wet sand, we would let
it drip down and form the closest thing to a hoodoo we have in
San Diego, drip castles! I was ready to see the real thing.

We drove into Bryce from our campground fifty miles
away. Having a general sense of the direction, we figured we
would recognize the park when we got there. A little distracted
by new sights, and with four kids in the back seat chanting,
"Are we there yet?" we reached our destination faster than we
had anticipated. There were gorgeous red rocks and towering

hoodoos. We parked at the Red Canyon Visitor Center, surprised by how few visitors there actually were. We had all of Bryce Canyon to ourselves! Back home I told our friends how beautiful it was and how we had hiked the entire Canyon. I couldn't wait to visit again.

When we returned the following year, we used the Maps app on my wife's iPhone to direct us. As it turns out, we never made it to Bryce Canyon on our first visit. We stopped thirteen miles short of where the historic hoodoos rested because I assumed that "Red Canyon" was just a name given by the locals to Bryce. Red Canyon is nice, but it isn't Bryce! As close as we were, we completely missed it.

The same thing happens all too often with the kingdom of Christ. Jesus's earliest recorded sermons began, "The time is fulfilled, and the kingdom of God is at hand; repent and believe in the gospel" (Mark 1:15). Something at hand is nearby, just up the road even. Imagine the excitement of Jesus's audience. For hundreds of years many have been crying out, "Are we there yet?" And now they had their answer. *We've almost arrived; the kingdom of God is just around the bend!* These were people tired of living under Rome's fat thumb. They were looking for a king who might turn the tables over on Gentile paganism and restore the kingdom to Israel. This expectation was so pervasive that Jesus's own disciples had a hard time escaping it (Acts 1:6).

Despite its nearness, many who heard Jesus's message completely missed the kingdom he preached. Nearby things are so easy to overlook. Like the car keys you spend fifteen minutes frantically searching for only to find them clenched in your fist. Today, as in Christ's day, people park short of or drive right by the realm of glory. This means that before we can pray *Your kingdom come*, we need to know what exactly we're looking for. Otherwise, we might just end up circling the Red Canyon, thinking all the while that we have reached Bryce.

God's Twofold Reign

In September of 2022, Queen Elizabeth II died after a seventy-year reign, making her the longest serving monarch in English history. I watched as her successor, King Charles III, was proclaimed king on live television. Trumpets blared as cries of "God save the king" rang out. It was a historic moment for the monarchy, and one which the world was privy to thanks to television cameras.

Unlike the Queen's successor, God as the Creator of all things never began to rule. He didn't have any predecessors before him, he simply *was* and *is*. Cyprian the bishop of Carthage wrote in the third century, "For when does God not reign, or when does that which always was, and shall never cease to be, begin?"[1] It's a good question, and it should cause us to wonder what's behind this particular petition, *Your kingdom come*. Isn't the kingly reign of God already here, and hasn't he been calling the shots since the moment he said, "Let there be light" in Genesis 1:3?

The answer is yes, but this only refers to one kind of God's rule. We can call this *God's universal rule* or *natural rule*. It refers to his kingship over all, which is his by virtue of his work of creation. The psalmist spoke of this rule in Psalm 103:19 when he said, "The LORD has established his throne in the heavens, and his kingdom rules over all." God's universal rule never increases or diminishes in the world, and it's exercised through God's works of providence. We might think of *providence* as a pious word for luck, but it's one of the most comforting realities in Scripture. God didn't just create the world and hit autopilot; he is actively governing and sustaining all his creatures and all their actions. God's acts of providence remind us that even when calamity strikes, God has not lost control. As King, he is guiding the course of human history in such a way that it magnifies his glory and tends toward our salvation.

Besides God's universal rule, we can also speak about his *special*, or *mediatorial*, *rule*. This rule focuses not so much on the providential sustaining of creation, but the bringing about of a redemptive new creation. This special manifestation of God's kingdom is seen wherever the Holy Spirit is raising the dead to life. Jesus told Nicodemus, "Unless one is born again he cannot see the kingdom of God" (John 3:3). It's *this* aspect of God's reign that we call down whenever we pray *Your kingdom come*.

While God is always King of creation, Jesus was endowed with a unique kingly authority after his resurrection (Matthew 28:18). His ascension into heaven culminated in what can only be described as the greatest coronation ceremony in history. Peter described this in his Pentecost sermon:

> "This Jesus God raised up, and of that we all are
> witnesses. Being therefore exalted at the right hand of
> God, and having received from the Father the promise
> of the Holy Spirit, he has poured out this that you
> yourselves are seeing and hearing. For David did not
> ascend into the heavens, but he himself says, "The
> Lord said to my Lord, sit at my right hand, until I
> make your enemies your footstool." Let all the house
> of Israel therefore know for certain that God has made
> him both Lord and Christ, this Jesus whom you cruci-
> fied." (Acts 2:32–36)

At his ascension, Jesus entered the courts of heaven as a conquering king (Revelation 5:5). The celestial hosts didn't cry out "God save the king!" But the king has saved *us*!

> "Worthy are you to take the scroll and to open its
> seals, for you were slain, and by your blood you ran-
> somed people for God from every tribe and language
> and people and nation, and you have made them a

kingdom and priests to our God, and they shall reign on the earth." (Revelation 5:9–10)

From heaven, Jesus rules his multiethnic, catholic kingdom. The word *catholic* is sometimes confused with Roman Catholic—but it simply means *universal*. The kingdom we pray for isn't associated with one nation like it was during the time of the Old Testament (Israel), but is composed of people from every nation. It's a worldwide rule that manifests itself wherever the charter of the kingdom, the gospel, is faithfully proclaimed. We might not be able to see our king now, but we can see the effect of his rule throughout the world, and even in our own lives.

What exactly is this kingdom? The best and most basic way to define it is the *new creation*. The Bible teaches that the world we currently live in—rife with sin and death—will one day be eclipsed by a new world. Peter said, "According to his promise we are waiting for new heavens and a new earth in which righteousness dwells" (2 Peter 3:13). Even now we see evidence that the winter of sin and death are coming to an end (1 John 2:8). We are, in fact, the flowers of the new creation, which have already begun to sprout and will one day fully bloom. Paul said, "If anyone is in Christ, he is a new creation. The old has passed away; behold, the new has come" (2 Corinthians 5:17).

This is why theologians sometimes speak of the kingdom as being *already* and *not yet*. Jesus's kingdom was mysteriously inaugurated during the time of his earthly ministry through preaching, performing miracles, casting out demons, and ultimately dying and rising again from the dead. Consider just a couple verses from the Gospels:

- "But if it is by the Spirit of God that I cast out demons, then the kingdom of God has come upon you" (Matthew 12:28; cf. Luke 11:20).

- "Being asked by the Pharisees when the kingdom of God would come, he answered them, 'The kingdom of God is not coming in ways that can be observed, nor will they say, "Look, here it is!" or "There!" for behold, the kingdom of God is in the midst of you'" (Luke 17:20–21).

So God's kingdom came with Jesus, but it's also coming in greater splendor. The continued presence of sin and death are constant reminders that Jesus is still in the process of subduing the earth (1 Corinthians 15:25–26). There's more to come of God's kingdom, not in terms of substance, but scope. The new creation believers experience now will one day be felt by the whole created order (Romans 8:22)! Until we reach that point—the point of consummation—we beseech God to restore all things by praying *Your kingdom come.*

To summarize, from the beginning of time God has been King of the cosmos with undiminished rule (God's universal reign), but throughout biblical history he's also ruled in a special way over his creatures to usher in the promise of a new creation (God's special reign). When Jesus came to earth, he brought this special kingdom reign with him, and he's been spreading it since the day he ascended into heaven. If you believe in Jesus, you yourself are a new creation! How should we look for God to answer practically the prayer *Your kingdom come?*

When Heaven Invades Earth

As far as I can tell, this prayer is answered in three ways. First, there's the kingdom's advancement *within us.* This happens when Jesus's reign expands in our hearts. Next, there's the kingdom's advancement *around us.* Here the focus is on the charter of the kingdom spreading beyond the walls of the church into hostile territory. Finally, there's the kingdom's advancement *ahead of us*—when the kingdom of God will be fully and finally realized at the second coming of Jesus. When we pray *Your kingdom come*, we can focus on any or all of these. Let's go a little deeper into each one and then conclude by thinking about who does the work of building the kingdom.

The kingdom within us

A few years back, I went to a conference for church planters where the focus was on difficult cities to reach in ministry. In between conference lectures, while attendees huddled in the lobby or at the lunch tables, conversations orbited around the challenges unique to each planter's context. For some, it was planting in inner-city neighborhoods that made reaching financial independence seem impossible. For others, it was planting in areas burned over by cultural Christianity and attempting to reach people who didn't think they needed Jesus. Each city had its own roadblocks to the gospel's progress.

One of the plenary talks titled "The Hardest Place to Reach" created a bit of a stir. Naturally, I think each of us felt like ours was the hardest city to reach, so we hoped for some outside confirmation. In the end, the talk focused on the fact that sometimes, the hardest place to reach is *our own heart*. You've probably heard the saying, "The longest distance in the world is the eighteen inches from your head to your heart." Think of your heart like a city that Jesus governs. Even though he's claimed it as his own, within our hearts there remain rebellious factions of sin and unbelief, areas we're either unaware of or that we try to cordon off from Christ's rule.

King David prayed, "Who can discern his errors? Declare me innocent from hidden faults" (Psalm 19:12). In this context, hidden faults aren't the sins we intentionally try to hide from God and others, but the ones hidden even to us. David's question—who can discern his errors?—highlights the struggle we each face to rightly assess our spiritual condition. When we pray *Your kingdom come*, we're asking Christ to beautify the dark alleys of our souls that remain dilapidated by sin, whether hidden or known.

Calvin described this in *Institutes of the Christian Religion*:

> God reigns where men, both by denial of themselves and by contempt of the world and of earthly life, pledge themselves to his righteousness in order to aspire to a heavenly life. . . . Therefore, no others keep a lawful order in this petition but those who *begin with themselves*, that is, to be cleansed of all corruptions that disturb the peaceful state of God's kingdom and sully its purity (emphasis added).[2]

When we trusted in Christ, God "delivered us from the domain of darkness and transferred us to the kingdom of his beloved Son" (Colossians 1:13). You are in Christ's kingdom, but the kingdom still needs to get more in you. As the Holy Spirit works in our lives, executing the rebel factions within our hearts, we experience the power of Christ's rule personally (Romans 8:13). This is sometimes what theologians call sanctification, that process of inward renewal whereby we are conformed more and more each day into the image of Christ.

Are there areas of your life that you know are in rebellion? Pray *Your kingdom come* with those areas in mind, asking Jesus to break the influence of the world and Satan, which still have a sway on your heart. The good news is even large rebel encampments are no match for the work of the Holy Spirit, and Jesus can see the rebel safe houses that are hidden from our perception.

The kingdom around us

The kingdom of God should spread from our hearts to our homes and communities. A prayer for the coming of the kingdom is a prayer for the advancement of the gospel through local and global missions. Remember that the king, Jesus, commissioned his followers to go into all the world and make disciples (Matthew 28:19), increasing the citizenship rolls of heaven. The book of Acts describes the unfolding of the church's mission in the first century, and it's clear from Luke's record there that prayer went hand in hand with preaching (Acts 4:29–31). This petition should therefore reinvigorate the church's missionary focus.

Calvin is again helpful here. He wrote, "Because the word of God is like a royal scepter, we are bidden here to entreat him to bring all men's minds and hearts into voluntary obedience to it. This happens when he manifests the working of his word through the secret inspiration of the Spirit."[3]

Note carefully *how* the kingdom of God advances among the hostile kingdoms of this world. Because it's not of this world (John 18:36), we shouldn't expect it to spread by worldly methods. God's kingdom comes not by way of coercion, but crucifixion. The kingdom's best ambassadors are disciples of Jesus who faithfully bear and share the message of the cross. The Spirit of the new creation uses the preaching of the cross to convict and convert sinners, thus enlarging the kingdom's borders. Calvin wrote, "For it is in this way that God wills to spread his kingdom."[4]

These ambassadors are sent by the church, and since the church is a manifestation of the new creation on earth, a prayer for the coming of the kingdom is also a prayer for the well-being of our churches. When Paul wrote to the church in Rome, he confronted them for dividing over dietary preferences. He was quick to remind them, "The kingdom of God is not a matter of eating and drinking but of righteousness and peace and joy in the Holy Spirit" (Romans 14:17). Churches that are well governed by Jesus's word and Spirit should exhibit this unity, peace, and righteousness. To the extent that they don't, they're poor reflections of God's rule. Therefore, we must continue to pray that the kingdom that shapes our hearts and advances throughout the world would manifest itself clearly in and through the ministry of the church.

Where do you long to see heaven invade the world around you? Is there an absence of the joy of Jesus and the peace of the Holy Spirit in your home? How about the community in which you live? Are there neighborhoods ravaged by drug abuse or blinded by affluence? When we pray *Your kingdom come*, we're praying that Christ's rule would bring healing where Satan has wreaked havoc. As you pray, imagine what the reign of Jesus would do in the lives of the people you love and the community you live in.

The kingdom ahead of us

One of the words used in early Christian worship was *Maranatha*. It's an Aramaic word made up of the words *Lord* (or our Lord) and *come*. Paul used it in the context of a rebuke in 1 Corinthians: "If anyone does not love the Lord, he is to be accursed. *Maranatha*" (16:22, NASB1995).

To pray *Your kingdom come* is another way of praying *Maranatha*. We long for the justice and righteousness that accompany the second coming of Jesus. Throughout Scripture, the arrival of God's kingdom was heralded as good news for the poor and oppressed people of God. On the flip side, it's terrifying news for the enemies of God's kingdom. Consider Paul's words to the Thessalonians:

> [Your persecutions are] evidence of the righteous judgment of God, that you may be considered worthy of the kingdom of God, for which you are suffering—since indeed God considers it just to repay with affliction those who afflict you, and to grant relief to you who are afflicted as well as to us, when the Lord

Jesus is revealed from heaven with his mighty angels
in flaming fire, inflicting vengeance on those who
do not know God and on those who do not obey the
gospel of our Lord Jesus. (2 Thessalonians 1:5–8)

As it relates to the world, this petition is double-edged. It's
both a cry for mercy, and a cry for justice. We long to see the
kingdom advance and the gospel embraced by those who hate
Christ. At the same time, we pray that God would curb injustice by restraining his enemies. We join the martyrs beneath
God's altar in heaven, who cried, "O Sovereign Lord, holy and
true, how long before you will judge and avenge our blood on
those who dwell on the earth?" (Revelation 6:10).

As we see the evil in the world, and long for the new creation, the groanings of *Maranatha—Your kingdom come*—well
up within us. We're reminded that the king who inaugurated
his kingdom is coming back to consummate it. Only then will
the fullness of the kingdom be realized.

Bricks in the Hands of Jesus

When it comes to the kingdom, we are first and foremost
bricks, not builders. Jesus is the one who builds and bestows
the kingdom. Consider these verses:

- Luke 12:32, "Fear not, little flock, for it is your Father's
  good pleasure to *give* you the kingdom."
- Luke 22:29, "I assign to you, as my Father assigned to
  me, a kingdom."
- Matthew 5:5, "Blessed are the meek, for they shall
  inherit the earth."
- Matthew 25:34, "Then the King will say to those on his
  right, 'Come, you who are blessed by my Father, inherit
  the kingdom prepared for you from the foundation of
  the world.'"

- Hebrews 12:28, "Therefore let us be grateful for receiving a kingdom that cannot be shaken, and thus let us offer to God acceptable worship, with reverence and awe."

Since the kingdom is a gift to be inherited, the gospel of the kingdom isn't "Get to work hammering!" Be wary of anyone who tells you to get to work building the kingdom because to the extent that *you* build it with your own hands, it won't be the kingdom of God (Daniel 2:34, cf. Hebrews 11:10). We pray *Your kingdom come* because the kingdom is something God gives, and he doesn't give it to the mighty who conquer in a worldly manner, but to the meek who take up their crosses and follow Jesus (Matthew 16:24).

Writing to exiled believers scattered across Asia Minor Peter said, "You yourselves like living stones are being built up as a spiritual house, to be a holy priesthood, to offer spiritual sacrifices acceptable to God through Jesus Christ" (1 Peter 2:5). As stones in God's universal temple, we've been quarried by the sword of the Spirit, washed clean by faith through the waters of baptism, and nourished by the body and blood of Jesus in the Lord's Supper.

So how can you know when you've arrived at the kingdom Jesus preached? Through the Holy Spirit's work of faith in your heart, you're made alive to see what the world so often overlooks. When you gather with other Christians to worship the King, you enter the sphere of kingdom operations. Each Sunday the church tastes the powers of the age to come—the not-yet of God's kingdom (Hebrews 6:5)—whetting our appetites for the feast that's ahead. As the powers of heaven continue to mold us, and the Word of God moves from our hearts to our homes, to the whole world, we rest knowing that we aren't just circling Zion; we've been made a part of the Holy Mountain itself.

A Prayer from the Past

Lord, we want to invite you to our homes. So we decorate them with giving to the needy, with prayers, with requests, and with vigils that focus unceasingly on the needs of others. These are the decorations of Christ the King. We are not ashamed then of having a humble house, if it has this kind of furniture. But the decorations that come from unstoppable greed are the enemy of Christ. May those of us who are rich not pride ourselves on having an expensive house. Rather let us hide our faces, turn away from greed, and seek the other kind of decoration. In so doing let us receive Christ in this life on earth, and there enjoy the eternal home, by the grace and love you have for us in Jesus Christ, to whom be glory and might, world without end, amen.

—John Chrysostom

Prayer Practices

1. What would be different in your life if God's kingdom took more ground in your heart? As you reflect on potential changes, pray for God's kingdom to come in specific ways to you personally. Try this for a month and take note throughout the month of how God is answering your prayers.

2. News and social media constantly put suffering and injustice throughout the world right in front of us. Think about some of the great injustices in our world and spend some time praying for the kingdom ahead of us. Try to make the laments of others your own as you pray *Maranatha*!

Questions for Discussion

1. What were some ways Jesus's first audience misunderstood the coming of the kingdom? Do you see some of those misunderstandings carried over in our day?
2. How does the kingdom of God advance in the world today?
3. Where is your focus with this petition in your own life: the kingdom within us, the kingdom around us, or the kingdom ahead of us?

Chapter Seven

Thy Will Be Done

There can now be no grander prayer than to wish that earthly things may be made equal with things heavenly: for what else is it to say "Thy will be done as in heaven so on earth," than to ask that men may be like angels, and that as God's will is ever fulfilled by them in heaven, so also all those who are on earth may do not their own but His will?

—John Cassian, fourth-century monastic

Orthodox priest Alexander Schmemann called the third petition of the Lord's Prayer the most difficult petition. He gave a series of radio talks to the former Soviet Union intended to challenge atheism as well as complacent faith, what he called *religiosity*. Why did he think this petition was the most difficult? Because "even the most ardent believer all too regularly, if not always, desires, expects, and asks from the God he claims to believe in that God would fulfill precisely his own will and not the will of God."[1] In other words, our inclination isn't to pray, *Thy will be done* but *My will be done*!

This led Fr. Schmemann to identify *Thy will be done* as the ultimate test of true faith. The petition shines a light within us, illuminating our own intentions in coming before God, and, at least according to the now-deceased priest, the genuineness of our faith.

It's interesting to note that soon after Jesus taught his disciples to pray in the Sermon on the Mount, he had something else to say about the will of God being done. In what may be the most sobering passage in the entire Bible, Jesus said the following:

> "Not everyone who says to me, 'Lord, Lord,' will enter the kingdom of heaven, but the one who does the will of my Father who is in heaven. On that day many will say to me, 'Lord, Lord, did we not prophesy in your name, and cast our demons in your name, and do many mighty works in your name?' And then I will declare to them, 'I never knew you; depart from me, you workers of lawlessness.'" (Matthew 7:21–23)

Jesus warned about those who say, "Lord, Lord!" but whose lives are characterized by the pursuit of lawlessness. Sure, they might have what Schmemann called religiosity. But they don't know Jesus, or as he puts it, *he didn't know them*. In the Bible, the word *know* speaks of intimacy in relationship. Jesus isn't claiming ignorance about their existence; rather, he's saying that they had no union with him. For all the works they could point to, prophesying, exorcisms, etc., they lacked true faith. True faith is the ground of Christian obedience.

Each time we pray *Your will be done*, we are asking for the strength to lay down our lives and take up our crosses in pursuit of Christ. But first things first: What exactly is the will of God?

Two Ways of Thinking about God's Will

Have you ever been faced with an important life decision where, between two options, both seemed pretty good? Often, we come to a fork in the road, and we'd like God to make our decision for us. "Tell me which one you choose, Lord!" I've noticed that when people talk about seeking God's will for their lives, they usually have something like this in mind. As we're confronted with a new challenge or opportunity, naturally we want God to make the way clear. In scenarios like these, God's will is something hidden that we're meant to discover. As we search, we can at times grow frustrated, wondering why God hasn't made his will clearer.

Here's the problem: we've confused God's *secret will* with his *revealed will*. As a result, we assume deciphering the will of God is sort of like cracking a code. It isn't! Clearing up this confusion is crucial to understanding what we're praying about in this petition.

Deuteronomy 29:29 explains,

> "The secret things belong to the LORD our God, but the things that are revealed belong to us and to our children forever, that we may do all the words of this law."

Note the distinction being made here: that which is secret versus that which is revealed or made known. The secret things belong to the Lord, not to us. What are the secret things? Usually here we're talking about God's eternal decree: what he has sovereignly determined will take place from all eternity. Paul told the Ephesians that God "works all things according to the counsel of his will" (Ephesians 1:11). Similarly, Psalm 33:11 says, "The counsel of the LORD stands forever, the plans of his heart to all generations."

As much as we might love access to God's decree, he hasn't granted it to us. David could say that all his days were written in a book when as yet there were none (Psalm 139:16), but he had no idea what each one of those future days would hold. Neither do we! When we pray for God's will to be done, we're not primarily asking for him to aid us in choosing between the red pill or the blue pill; we're asking him to grant us obedience to his *revealed will*. We're saying, "Lord, no matter what tomorrow brings, help me to obey what you've called me to."

God's revealed will isn't just for us; it's also for our children! If anything, this should remind us that finding the will of God *isn't* like solving a calculus problem. God's revealed will is clearly summarized for us in his holy law. Remember, Jesus said that the false teachers in Matthew 7 didn't do the will of God because they practiced *lawlessness*. The revealed will of God helps us understand our personal duty before the Lord, and God isn't cryptic about this. "You have commanded your precepts to be kept diligently" (Psalm 119:4). With clarity the Scriptures teach what we're to believe about God and what duties he requires of us.

How should these duties happen? Jesus added to this petition an example—*on earth as it is in heaven* (Matthew 6:10b). Throughout the Bible we see the heavenly bodies and the heavenly beings eager to obey the commands of God. The heavenly bodies refer to the stars and planets above. Consider their compliance with the commands of God:

- "He made the moon to mark the seasons; the sun knows its time for setting" (Psalm 104:19).
- "The heavens declare the glory of God, and the sky above proclaims his handiwork. Day to day pours out speech, and night to night reveals knowledge" (Psalm 19:1–2).

The sun and moon know the purposes for which they were created. They faithfully do their jobs, testifying of the power of the Creator to anyone willing to listen (Romans 1:20). Similarly, the heavenly beings—angels—are sent by God to accomplish his will.

- "Bless the LORD, O you his angels, you mighty ones who do his word, obeying the voice of his word! Bless the LORD, all his hosts, his ministers, who do his will" (Psalm 103:20–21).
- "For he will command his angels concerning you to guard you in all your ways" (Psalm 91:11).
- "Are they [the angels] not all ministering spirits sent out to serve for the sake of those who are to inherit salvation?" (Hebrews 1:14).

The angels of heaven are servants of God accomplishing his will in the world. When we pray *Your will be done on earth as it is in heaven*, it's as if we're saying, *God, make me like the sun, which rises and sets at your command. Make me like the stars, which don't stop proclaiming your greatness. Like the angels, who are eager to obey your voice and carry out your will.* Perhaps now we can see why some have stressed the difficulty of this petition. As beautiful as heavenly obedience sounds, who would say that such an obedience was theirs? What does it look like for this prayer to be answered in the lives of those who struggle to obey God's commands—people like us?

Two Ways of Fulfilling God's Will

In the early days of the Protestant Reformation, a controversy arose which came to be called the Antinomian Controversy. The word *antinomian* is a compound word from two Greek words, which woodenly translated means "against law." Antinomians broadly defined are those who set aside the relevance of God's law for the life of the believer. Recognizing how important this question was to biblical fidelity, Martin Luther engaged in a series of disputations against the antinomians. Appealing to Scripture, he showed *how* the will of God is to be fulfilled in the life of the believer.

First, Luther demonstrated that because we are united to Jesus Christ by faith, the law of God *has been perfectly fulfilled* in us by Jesus. Second, he taught that in Christ, God has filled us with his Spirit so that we might *imperfectly begin to fulfill the righteous requirements of God's law.* He wrote the following:

> Therefore, since we cannot fulfill the Law because of the sin reigning in our flesh and holding it captive, Christ came and killed that sin by sin—that is, by the sacrifice made for sin—that in this way the righteousness required by the Law might be fulfilled in us: first, by way of imputation, and then formally as well [that is, in reality]—yet this is not of ourselves [cf. Eph. 2:8] but by the grace of God, who sent His Son in the flesh. He gives the Spirit to those who believe these things so that they begin to hate sin sincerely; to recognize the immense, incomprehensible, and ineffable gift; to give thanks to God for it; to love, worship, and call on God; and to expect everything from Him. For if He gave up His Son—gave Him up for sins—He will surely also give us all things with Him [Rom. 8:32].[2]

Throughout his disputations, Luther makes clear that Jesus Christ has perfectly fulfilled the law in our place. Through imputation—the crediting to our account of Jesus's perfect obedience—we therefore stand before God justified. This is the foundation for our own obedience to the will of God. Now, as the justified in Christ, we render true obedience to the commandments of God, albeit imperfectly. This is precisely what the apostle Paul was getting at when he wrote the following to the Romans:

> For God has done what the law, weakened by the flesh, could not do. By sending his own Son in the likeness of sinful flesh and for sin, he condemned sin

in the flesh, in order that the righteous requirement of
the law might be fulfilled in us, who walk not according to the flesh but according to the Spirit. (Romans
8:3–4)

This is foundational for understanding what we mean
when we say *Your will be done*. If the will in question is God's
revealed will, then we're praying that the duties God requires
of humanity would be joyfully embraced. Since all have sinned
and fallen short of the glory of God, we recognize that this
cannot be realized apart from Jesus Christ! Again, Luther
agrees: "So the demand of the Law is sad, hateful, and impossible for those outside of Christ. On the other hand, for those
under Christ, it begins to become a delight, even possible."[3]
The perfect obedience of Christ that justifies us, securing our
eternal redemption, becomes the means through which, by the
Spirit, we begin to delight in God's will over our own. Our
Lord himself was familiar with this struggle.

Two Wills of the God-Man

Because sin has affected every facet of human nature, our wills
bend inward. This is *why* the third petition is impossible to
pray apart from the grace of God. The Son of God and eternal
Word of the Father came to earth and became incarnate in
part so that our crippled wills might be restored. This was the
subject of a controversy that preceded Luther's time, known as
the Monothelite controversy. Monothelite (like antinomian) is
a compound Greek word that means "one will."

Between the fifth and seventh centuries, there was an
increased focus on the nature of Christ's action and will.
Because there's one will in God the Holy Trinity (grounded
in the reality of God's singular essence), some made the case
that our Lord Jesus possessed only one divine will. As theo-
logically hairsplitting as this might seem at first, it's crucial to

the salvation of humanity. Since our human wills are fallen through sin, it was necessary for the Son of God to assume the totality of human nature, including a human will. Hebrews tells us that Jesus "had to be made like his brothers in every respect, so that he might become a merciful and faithful high priest in the service of God" (Hebrews 2:17). It's clear, then, that the incarnate Son possessed two wills: human and divine.

This is why Jesus could pray as he did, "For I have come down from heaven, not to do my own will but the will of him who sent me" (John 6:38). Perhaps no passage was more important to this debate than Jesus's prayer in the garden of Gethsemane prior to his crucifixion, "Father, if you are willing, remove this cup from me. Nevertheless, not my will, but yours, be done" (Luke 22:42). In the cry of Gethsemane, we hear the echo of the third petition coming from Jesus's own mouth: *Thy will be done.* Does this mean the two wills of the God-Man are in conflict? No. Answering this question, John of Damascus wrote the following:

> In the Father and Son and Holy Ghost we discover the identity of nature from the identity of the operation and the will. In the divine Incarnation, on the other hand, we discover the difference in nature from the difference of the wills and operations, and knowing the difference of the natures we confess the difference of the wills and operations. For, just as the number of the natures piously understood and declared to belong to one and the same Christ does not divide this one Christ, but shows that the difference of the natures is maintained even in the union, neither does the number of the wills and operations belonging substantially to his natures introduce any division—God forbid—*for in both of his natures he wills and acts for our salvation* (emphasis added).[4]

In layman's terms, the two wills of the incarnate Son of God work in concert for your redemption. Not only do we follow Jesus in praying *Thy will be done*, but the answer to this prayer is possible solely because the Son paved the way for the restoration of our wills through his incarnation. He fulfilled all the righteous requirements of the Law—God's revealed will— so that we might be restored fully. The author to the Hebrews wrote,

> Consequently, when Christ came into the world, he said, "Sacrifices and offerings you have not desired, but a body you have prepared for me; in burnt offerings and sin offerings you have taken no pleasure. Then I said, 'Behold, I have come to do you will, O God, as it is written of me in the scroll of the book.'" (Hebrews 10:5–7)

Alexander Schmemann was right: this petition is the most difficult. In fact, perfect obedience to the law of God isn't just difficult for sinful humanity; it's *impossible*. From heaven God saw us, bent inward and serving ourselves. We hadn't just failed to do what he asked, but on many occasions, we did the very opposite, breaking God's revealed will time and time again. What was a loving God to do? Filled with compassion, he sent the Word in our humanity to do the very thing he commanded us to pray for: the Father's will. In Jesus, all our transgressions are forgiven, and we are enabled not only to pray for but to pursue the will of God as men and women renewed by the Holy Spirit. Through Jesus then let us pray: *Thy will be done!*

A Prayer from the Past

Lord, I love you above all other things. You are the one I seek. You are the one I follow. You are the one I am ready to serve. I want to dwell under your rule, for you alone reign. Command me as you will, but heal and open my eyes to see your wonders. And drive all foolishness and pride from me. Give me wisdom to understand you, and teach me where to look to see you. Then I will gladly do what you command. Amen.

—AUGUSTINE OF HIPPO

Prayer Practices

1. Reflect on the parts of God's revealed will that you have the most difficulty with. It could be a particular commandment you have a hard time obeying. Every time you pray *Your will be done*, add: *in helping me to follow you with X*. Keep track of how you see the Lord answering this specific request.

2. Read Micah 6, noting God's will for his people, especially as expressed in verse 8. Spend some time prayerfully considering what the pursuit of justice, love of mercy, and call to humility might look like in your own life.

Questions for Discussion

1. What's the difference between God's hidden and revealed will? Do you ever find yourself trying to figure out the former while neglecting the latter?

2. Have you ever found yourself at a metaphorical fork in the road and prayed, *God, what should I do?* In situations like those, what helpful ways of discerning God's will factor in Scripture and wisdom?

3. Since no one can perfectly obey God's law, what is the ground for our assurance of salvation?

Chapter Eight

Give Us This Day Our Daily Bread

But mark, I pray thee, how even in things that are bodily, that which is spiritual abounds. For it is neither for riches, nor for delicate living, nor for costly raiment, nor for any other such thing, but for bread only, that he hath commanded us to make our prayer.

—John Chrysostom

What's the first thing you do when you get up in the morning? A 2019 study exploring the routines of Americans looking to start their day on a positive note found that 50 percent of us prioritize one thing above everything else: coffee! I'm among those who appreciate it. When struck by the forenoon panic induced by the discovery of depleted coffee grounds, we jet to Starbucks before the kids realize the night is over. Without caffeine, the sun just doesn't seem to rise the same way (even in southern California).

After coffee, many listed exercise as the next component for a good day's start. Of course, there's also the things we just sort of take for granted—brushing your teeth, taking a shower, and getting clothes on, which are things you probably should do before stepping out the door. (I know, showers are debatable here, but not for me.) Between the stuff you'd like to accomplish in the morning, and the stuff you simply can't leave undone, where do you prioritize prayer?

I spent some time back in chapter 3 unpacking the word *daily* that Jesus used here. It may be helpful for you to go back and review the introductory section there, but to summarize, the word assumes we're to begin each day looking to God in humble reliance. Jesus confirms this just a little later in the Sermon on the Mount, "Do not be anxious about tomorrow, for tomorrow will be anxious for itself. Sufficient for the day is its own trouble" (Matthew 6:34). This petition teaches us that we depend upon God for our physical needs as much as our spiritual ones. We could even take that one step further: our physical needs are foundational to our spiritual ones!

The Bread That Comes from the Earth

One of our favorite things to do as a family is go pier fishing. In all honesty, I'm not a very good fisherman. Equipped with a couple of the cheapest poles I could find on Amazon and frozen shrimp from SquidCo. Fishing, a bait shop near my house, we head to the pier, hoping our kids get the pleasure of reeling in a fish. Most days we catch something, a stingray, even an octopus once! We always toss them back into the bay though. For us, fishing is a fun way to teach our kids the virtue of waiting. For others, fishing is a livelihood. Growing up in the city, I've never known the pressure of needing to grow or catch food to survive. You probably haven't either. This wasn't true for many people living near Jesus.

Did you know that most of the population in Jesus's day worked in some kind of food production? Jews in Palestine were primarily engaged in agriculture, according to the historian Josephus.[1] People were occupied with growing and harvesting olives, grapes, wheat, barley, and fishing where possible. It makes sense that so many of Jesus's teachings used agricultural illustrations and many of his earliest disciples were fishermen.

When you're so close to the catch that your life depends on it, the prayer for daily bread takes on new importance. Imagine a first-century hunter or fisherman praying that God would supply the next deer or trout. For many of us, food is so accessible that we take this petition for granted. We understand that we need God's help for forgiveness, but we think we have the daily bread part covered.

I grew up watching *The Simpsons*, an animated sitcom that portrays American life satirically. There's Homer, the bald father depicted as somewhat of a dolt, Marge the stereotypical housewife, and their three children, Bart, Lisa, and Maggie. Bart is a skateboarding rebel who is usually out causing trouble. In one episode he's asked to give thanks before supper in front of Homer's boss (Mr. Burns) and he shocks the table when he prays, "Dear God, we pay for all this stuff ourselves so thanks for nothing!" Yikes!

Of course, we'd never say it aloud, but I'm afraid many of us pray this petition without believing we're as dependent upon God as Jesus suggests. We can look disdainfully at the woman holding a cardboard sign and begging for bread, incapable of imagining ourselves as needy as she is. The truth is that we're beggars with hands outstretched to a gracious God. This reality gripped Martin Luther shortly before his death, who after years of being used mightily by God scribbled some of his last words onto a piece of paper, "We are beggars. This is true."[2] The more we become aware of our dependence upon God, the less we'll slip into the foolish ways of thinking that keep us from prayer:

- I don't need to depend on anyone.
- My success is solely attributed to my hard work and sacrifice.
- I earned the things I enjoy before me.

While our mouths repeat the words *Give us this day our daily bread*, our hearts cry out *Dear God, I worked for all this stuff myself—but thanks anyway.*

How might your prayer life change if you really believed God was the source of even your most basic daily needs? Perhaps thanksgiving before meals would become less rote. Maybe prayer would move from the list of things you'd like to do each morning to the list of things you wouldn't dream of leaving undone! We make the mistake of thinking that we depend upon God for the big spiritual stuff—salvation from sin, the Holy Spirit, miraculous healing, etc.—but when it comes to the day-to-day grind, we're in control. God gives spiritual blessings, but I'm the source of bread!

John Calvin gave a sobering warning about this kind of thinking. He wrote the following:

> Those who, not content with daily bread but panting after countless things with unbridled desire, or sated with their abundance, or carefree in their piled-up riches, supplicate God with this prayer are but mocking him. For the first ones ask him what they do not wish to receive, indeed, what they utterly abominate—namely, mere daily bread—and as much as possible cover up before God their propensity to greed, while true prayer ought to pour out before him the whole mind itself and whatever lies hidden within. But others ask of him what they least expect, that is, *what they think they have within themselves* (emphasis added).[3]

We do well to remember Moses's admonition to the people entering the Promised Land, "Beware lest you say in your heart, 'My power and the might of my hand have gotten me this wealth.' You shall remember the LORD your God, for it is he who gives you power to get wealth, that he may confirm his covenant that he swore to your fathers, as it is this day"

(Deuteronomy 8:17–18). In other words, God is just as much the source of your physical blessings as he is your spiritual ones. You might be a hard worker, but God gives the strength. At any moment pride threatens to render us as incapable as Nebuchadnezzar during his binge in the open field (Daniel 4:28–33).

The failure to see this leads to what I call common-grace Pelagianism. Admittedly, I'm stringing those words together in a way that's unusual, so let me explain. Common grace is the goodness of God that's common to all humanity. Jesus said that God "makes his sun rise on the evil and on the good, and sends rain on the just and on the unjust" (Matthew 5:45). Temporal provisions like physical bread are gifts that come to believers and unbelievers alike—but God is still their source (see also Acts 14:17).

Pelagianism was a fifth-century heresy that had to do not so much with *common* but *saving* grace. It was the idea that mankind didn't need the grace of God to be saved. Like Adam, we are born with a clean slate, able to pull ourselves up by spiritual bootstraps to achieve perfection (so Pelagius thought!). Of course, the view was rejected as heresy, and for good reason. Paul said, "For by grace you have been saved through faith. And this is not your own doing; it is the gift of God, not a result of works, so that no one may boast" (Ephesians 2:8–9).

So what is common-grace Pelagianism? It's the idea that you need God for saving grace, but not for your next meal. The truth is that you need him for both, just in different ways. Realizing this helps us not to take for granted the everyday gifts of God that we tend to overlook, like breakfast or chocolate cake.

Dutch missionary Andrew van der Bijl, or Brother Andrew as he was best known, told how God taught him to trust him for his physical needs. First, it was through observing the generosity of a kind couple, the Hopkinses.

I saw God meet their practical needs in the most
unusual ways. Never once did I see anyone go hungry
or coatless from their house. It wasn't that they had
money. From the profits of Mr. Hopkins' construction business they kept just enough to supply their
own modest needs. Strangers—such as myself and
the beggars and streetwalkers and drunks who passed
continually through their doors—had to be fed by
God. And he never failed.[4]

Soon after, Andrew would experience God's daily bread
provision even more personally. As a seminarian he received the
assignment of a four-week evangelistic training trip. Sent out
with only a one-pound banknote with which to travel through
Scotland, he and his team were expected to pay for their own
transportation, lodging, food, rental halls (for Bible lessons),
and even refreshments for the meetings! Moreover, they were
expected to return after four weeks able to pay the one pound
back! Forbidden from panhandling, they were forced to trust
God for their daily necessities.

God gave them just enough each day to get by via "ran-
dom" gifts in the post from family members or churches they
had visited in the past. The most memorable instance came
when his team had planned a gathering in Edinburgh. They
had attracted a group of young people with the promise of
tea and cake. Of course, they had money for neither! Their
last penny had gone to the fee for the hall where they would
be meeting. After much prayer, it looked like this would be a
cakeless tea—a true scandal for the Scottish boys, according to
Andrew! Then, fifteen minutes before the event, the doorbell
rang.

All of us together ran to the big front entrance,
and there was the postman. In his hand was a large
box . . . I took the package and carefully unwrapped

it. Off came the twine. Off came the brown outside paper. Inside, there was no note—only a large white box. Deep in my soul I knew that I could afford the drama of lifting the lid slowly. As I did, there, in perfect condition, to be admired by five sets of wondering eyes, was an enormous, glistening, moist, chocolate cake.[5]

It was a gift from the heavenly Father, baked by the hands of Mrs. Hopkins.

I have my own "chocolate cake stories," and I trust you do as well. We must not forget that even when God's provision arrives earlier than fifteen minutes before the party is set to begin, or the rent is due, it's still God's provision. The bona fide tales we can share serve as personal memorials, teaching us that God cares about our temporal needs just as he does our spiritual well-being. And, as I alluded to earlier, the sustaining of our physical life paves the way for our spiritual development. In other words, we can't sever the body from the spirit (as we discussed in chapter 2).

In his treatise, the *Enchiridion: On Faith, Hope, and Love*, St. Augustine noted how the petitions in the Lord's Prayer relate to both eternal and temporal goods. The temporal goods (like daily bread) are necessary in some sense for obtaining the eternal goods.[6] This correlation was also noted by St. Thomas Aquinas, who wrote, "Now it is lawful to desire temporal things, not indeed principally, by placing our end therein, but as helps whereby we are assisted in tending towards beatitude . . . "[7] The physical blessings we ask God for are gifts we can enjoy that should assist us in our relationship with God. They aren't to be sought as an "end," in other words, something we put our ultimate hope in. That would be to idolize the gift instead of worshipping the Giver. Nevertheless, we can't miss that God encourages us to ask for his temporal blessings with the hope that through them, we might better serve him.

This was precisely how Agur, the author of Proverbs 30, prayed to the Lord:

> Two things I ask of you; deny them not to me before I die: Remove far from me falsehood and lying; give me neither poverty nor riches; feed me with the food that is needful for me, lest I be full and deny you and say, "Who is the LORD?" or lest I be poor and steal and profane the name of my God. (Proverbs 30:7–9)

Agur asks for just enough daily bread to sustain him. The modesty of his request helps us to think twice about the kinds of physical blessings we pray for. Are we seeking God for things which, if he gave them to us, would lead us to say, "Who is the LORD?" When God says no to our prayer for some physical good, it's not because he's stingy or doesn't love us. Were God to grant every temporal blessing we requested, the results could very well be spiritually disastrous! Rather than growing frustrated with God for not giving us the rope with which to hang ourselves (spiritually speaking), we ought to seek God for whatever temporal blessings he sees fit to give us that increase our love for him and our neighbors.

I'm not saying that having more than enough bread for today is somehow evil. We can be evil through misuse of God's gifts, but the gifts themselves are good! The idea that physical blessings need to be avoided at all costs verges onto the opposing traffic of another ancient heresy known as Gnosticism.

The Gnostics were hyper-spiritual mystics that believed the cosmic redemption of our spirits would come through the acquisition of secret knowledge.[8] According to them, matter (like our physical bodies) was corrupt and something to escape from, rather than redeem. They minimized the created goodness of the physical world, leading to a denial of doctrines like the incarnation of the Son of God, Jesus. After all, if matter is evil, then why would God assume and bless humanity by taking a body to himself? To pray for bread to sustain our physical bodies and to receive it as a good gift from God displaces the unbiblical ideas that suggest God doesn't care for the physical world.

Now, you may not be a common-grace Pelagian, but do you struggle with diet Gnosticism? It's the watered-down version of the ancient heresy. Instead of trusting in yourself for your physical needs, you pit the physical world against the spiritual one. You see the body and "things" as roadblocks to vibrant spirituality, rather than as gifts from God.

I spoke with a young woman recently who was having difficulty enjoying anything in life that didn't fall under the umbrella of churchy activities. When she was reading her Bible or praying, she felt loved and accepted by God. But the moment she found herself enjoying anything outside of the "spiritual," she experienced crushing guilt. She felt that enjoying this world—food, music, or wine—was somehow inherently evil. That's diet Gnosticism! A proper understanding of daily bread—our physical needs—sees this world as something to enjoy, not abuse or abstain from. Paul warned Timothy that false teachers would come into the church "who forbid marriage and require abstinence from foods that God created to be received with thanksgiving by those who believe and know the truth" (1 Timothy 4:3). Then, only two chapters later, he instructed, "As for the rich in this present age, charge them not to be haughty, nor to set their hopes on the uncertainty of riches, but on God, who richly provides us with everything to enjoy" (1 Timothy 6:17).

What are the big takeaways? First, you're far more dependent upon God than you thought you were. The next meal you enjoy is a gratuitous gift sourced from the Father above (James 1:17; 1 Timothy 4:4–5). This means that instead of being common-grace Pelagians, we should ask God with humility to supply our basic necessities each day and then receive them with thanks. Second, the transition we've encountered at this stage in the Lord's Prayer, from God's glory to our needs, shows us that God cares about our day-to-day lives. Christianity isn't a gnostic religion, prioritizing the unseen realm without concern for the physical creation. God gives us bread and every other temporal blessing for our nourishment and joy. God cares about chocolate cake!

The Bread That Comes from Heaven

While I was in college, I had a Christian professor who invited me and several of my friends to his home for dinner. The food was excellent—meat, potatoes, salad, all seared, mashed, and tossed to perfection. As we finished, the professor looked around the table with a smirk and asked, "Now are you ready for the real feast?" Of course, I thought he was talking about chocolate cake. Just then, from beneath the table he pulled out a box that wasn't near the size you would hope it to be to contain a cake. He opened it, and handing each of us a note card, he said, "Let's go around the table; I'll start!" He looked down and began reading, "The steadfast love of the LORD never ceases; his mercies never come to an end; they are new every morning; great is your faithfulness" (Lamentations 3:22–23). "Mmmm!" he sighed contentedly, as if he had just bitten into a delicious steak. "Now you go." We each took turns reading and discussing different passages from the Bible. We talked and laughed and chewed upon the Word of God together. There, in his home around the table, he was giving us another lesson: God's Word is your true meat and drink.

God taught the Israelites this in the wilderness. A prayer for daily bread hearkens us back to Exodus 16 where God promised to give his people bread, "a day's portion every day" (Exodus 16:4). Their physical dependence upon God in the wilderness was supposed to teach them a spiritual truth. Moses explained the divine lesson in Deuteronomy 8:3: "And he humbled you and let you hunger and fed you with manna, which you did not know, nor did your fathers know, that he might make you know that man does not live by bread alone, but man lives by every word that comes from the mouth of the LORD."

When we come to the New Testament, we find that Jesus uses this story of God's daily bread provision to point to himself. John records, "'For the bread of God is he who comes down from heaven and gives life to the world.' . . . Jesus said to them, 'I am the bread of life; whoever comes to me shall not hunger, and whoever believes in me shall never thirst'" (John 6:33, 35).

The provision of physical bread is not an end in and of itself; rather it is meant to raise our minds up to Jesus, the true Bread from heaven who nourishes us with everlasting life. We weren't created merely to enjoy the world we inhabit, but through creation to look upon our Creator. We see him most clearly in signs whereby he exhibits to us the grace of salvation, like baptism and Holy Communion. It's not a coincidence that in the history of the church, many have seen in this petition an allusion to the Lord's Supper. Just like our physical bodies need bread to survive, our spiritual vitality is dependent on our being united to Jesus. He is the vine, and we are the branches.

Tertullian wrote,

> We should understand "Give us this day, our daily bread" better in a spiritual sense. For Christ is our bread, because Christ is life and bread is life. "I am," he said, "The bread of life." And a little earlier, "The bread is the word of the living God who came down from the heavens" (Jn. 6:48). Then, because his body is accounted bread: "This is my body" (Mt. 26:26; 1 Cor. 11:24). Therefore, when we ask for our daily bread, we are asking that we should perpetually be in

Christ and that we should not be separated from his body.[9]

God loves the physical world so much that he imbues it with spiritual significance. In the Lord's Supper, we experience heavenly grace through earthly bread. So we can see this petition as a prayer for our daily physical and spiritual needs. The God we depend on for these things is happy to give them to us. "Which one of you," Jesus said, "if his son asks him for bread, will give him a stone? Or if he asks for a fish, will give him a serpent? If you then, who are evil, know how to give good gifts to your children, how much more will your Father who is in heaven give good things to those who ask him!" (Matthew 7:9–11).

When we approach God each morning with our needs, we shouldn't conceive of him as frustrated or stingy. He's the good Father who provides everything we need for life *and* godliness (2 Peter 1:3). Let's open our eyes each morning and say, "Give us today our daily bread."

A Prayer from the Past

O Lord, in whom is the source and inexhaustible fountain of all good things, pour out thy blessing upon us, and sanctify to our use the meat and drink which are the gifts of thy kindness towards us, that we, using them soberly and frugally as thou enjoinest, may eat with a pure conscience. Grant, also, that we may always both with true heartfelt gratitude acknowledge, and with our lips proclaim thee our Father and the giver of all good, and, while enjoying bodily nourishment, aspire with special longing of heart after the bread of thy doctrine, by which our souls may be nourished in the hope of eternal life, through Christ our Lord. Amen.

—John Calvin, sixteenth-century Christian theologian and reformer

Prayer Practices

1. Make a list of the physical blessings you often take for granted. This could be your health, where you live, your job, family members, or friends. Once you have your list, imagine how your life would be different if you *didn't* have each one. Spend some time thanking God for his daily bread provision in your life.

2. If you don't have a routine of morning prayer, devote this week to trying to incorporate a brief prayer for the day somewhere alongside making coffee or brushing your teeth. Talk to a friend about your morning schedule and ask them to hold you accountable in starting each day with prayer.

Questions for Discussion

1. Do you take the prayer for daily bread for granted?
2. Do you have a personal "chocolate cake provision" story you could share?
3. What negative perceptions might you have about the created world?
4. What are some reasons we're tempted to pit God's creation against spirituality?

Chapter Nine

Forgive Us Our Debts

Lest anyone be self-satisfied, thinking himself innocent, and should perish once again because of his
boasting, he is informed and instructed daily that he
is a sinner, being commanded to make prayer daily on
account of his sins.

—St. Cyprian, third-century
bishop of Carthage

In California where I live, people are very familiar with the
idea of debt. If you're a homeowner, debt is basically inescap-
able. *USA Today* had an article in June of 2019 titled, "How
Much Mortgage Debt Does Your State Have? Two States are
Far and Away Above the Rest." California was number one on
that list with an average mortgage debt of $347,652.[1] Things
can't be much better today since the median home value has
jumped $250,000 since that article came out.

If you went to college around here, you graduated with an
average of $37,000 in school debt. In April of 2022, Califor-
nians had piled up over $140 billion in student loans.[2] Auto-
mobile debt hovers around $25,000[3]; and when it comes to
credit card debt, Californians have on average between $5,000
and 6,000.[4]

You don't have to live in California to be familiar with debt though. The average consumer debt for Americans is nearly $100,000.[5] I know, the news isn't all that encouraging, but I bring it up to point out that we are in a unique position to understand Jesus's words in this petition, *forgive us our debts, as we forgive our debtors.*

The Hebrews frowned upon debt. The Law of Moses had restrictions on loans that were meant to protect the poor from being taken advantage of. Exodus 22:25 says, "If you lend money to any of my people with you who is poor, you shall not be like a moneylender to him, and you shall not exact interest from him" (see also Deuteronomy 23:19–20). The root of the Hebrew word for interest, or usury, *neshekh,* can also mean to bite (Leviticus 25:36 cf. Genesis 49:17; Numbers 21:8; Amos 5:19). Debt, like sin, eats away at you and will consume you if left unchecked.

The Greco-Roman culture didn't have the strict regulations on debt that the Mosaic Law did, making extortion a real problem in Jesus's day. Our Lord could use debt as a picture in his teachings because it was a part of people's everyday experience (Matthew 18:23–34; Luke 12:57–59; 16:1–9).

The Biting Nature of Sin

It's the sins we sometimes treat as cute and continue to nurse that end up killing us. A man in Harlem, New York, made national news back in 2003 when it was discovered that he had been raising a tiger in his tiny apartment. He was a thirty-one-year-old construction worker who bought the tiger as a cub and began bottle-feeding it. The tiger, Ming, soon grew to require a diet of twenty pounds of chicken thighs per day. In less than three years, the Siberian-Bengal mix was between four hundred and five hundred pounds!

Things fell apart when the man sought medical attention after being bit by Ming. Doctors were skeptical of his story that a pit bull had bitten him due to the size of the bite radius on his leg. Somehow this man was able to hide a tiger without his neighbors or the housing authority ever taking notice. He nursed it until it became something he couldn't control—and it almost killed him.

Sin is like a tiger crouching at your door, and it desires to bite you to death (Genesis 4:7). You can nurse it, thinking it's cute or harmless, but in the end it grows to an unmanageable size. Because of this, you must take the consuming nature of sin seriously. This is precisely what Jesus did by likening sin to a debt that devours. The analogy between debt and sin reveals that each of us owes something to God, that sin collects interest, and that our only hope is God's debt forgiveness.

We owe God

Whether you'd identify yourself as a Christian or not, the Bible teaches that all humanity owes God the glory that is due to him as Creator. While mankind can see God's creative genius in the beauty of the visible world, we fail to "pay up" accordingly (Romans 1:21). Hoarding this glory for ourselves, or giving it to others, we commit what the Bible calls *idolatry*. Whenever you give your worship—heartfelt devotion and trust—to something other than God, you compound the debt of sin.

Believers in Jesus Christ are also debtors to God as those who have been redeemed, "bought back" by his divine grace. Though we had rebelled, God didn't turn his back on humanity, but he pursued us in love. The God you didn't love loved you (Romans 5:8). It was through this love that he forgave your sins, justified you, and adopted you into his family. Considering these glorious realities, Paul could say, "So then, brothers, we are debtors, not to the flesh, to live according to the flesh" (Romans 8:12).

A prayer from the ancient Christian liturgy of John Chrysostom prior to celebrating communion puts it beautifully:

> You brought us out of nothing into being, and when
> we had fallen away, you raised us up again. You left
> nothing undone until you had led us up to heaven and
> granted us your kingdom which is to come. For all
> these things we thank you . . .

As we meditate on God's goodness to us in creation and salvation, we ought to respond by giving him the worship and thanksgiving that are rightly owed to him. This isn't a payment made to earn God's mercy, but the proper response for having truly experienced it.

Before moving on, I think it's important to mention that most of us owed a larger spiritual debt than we could even conceive of. Jesus illustrated this in the parable of the unforgiving servant (Matthew 18:23–35). He told the story of a king (representative of God) who forgave one of his servants (representative of us) a debt of 10,000 talents. In the economy of Christ's day, one talent was an enormous sum, equal to around 6,000 denarii. One denarius was the common wage for a day of labor, which means this subject owed the equivalent of 60 million days, or 164,274 years of hard work!

Our debts are doubled when we realize that sin isn't just the bad stuff we do; it's also the good things we fail to do. God's law doesn't just prohibit immorality; it calls us to love God perfectly and our neighbor as ourselves (Mark 12:30–31). When we tally up our sins of neglect together with our blatant transgressions, we say with the psalmist, "For evils have encompassed me beyond number; my iniquities have overtaken me, and I cannot see; they are more than the hairs of my head; my heart fails me" (Psalm 40:12). The debt owed is insurmountable, but for the grace of God.

Sin collects interest

I mentioned already that the Jews weren't too keen on interest rates, but the Romans didn't have a problem with them. You're probably familiar with this concept if you have a credit card or a student loan. You want a low interest rate because the higher your rate, the quicker your debt will grow if it isn't paid off.

Do you know what the highest interest rate ever on a credit card was? 79.9%! That was the rate for the old First Premier Bank credit card (which is no longer available). The card was for people who had bad credit, and the interest rate was crippling. Debts don't just go away when they're ignored; instead, they collect interest and grow. *Sin functions the exact same way.* Sin that we just try to brush under the rug or forget about is sin collecting interest. Slowly, but surely, it's doing its work.

When I was a little boy, I thought I had a clever way of disposing of the foods I didn't want to eat during dinner. When my mother wasn't watching, I'd hide them around the house. Broccoli in the couch cushions doesn't disappear though—it putrefies! You can get away with hiding your dinner for a while, but over time it begins to stink up the whole house and call out from the crevasses where it's been concealed. You can only hide your sins for so long before the rot begins to expose itself. Apart from confession, the problem only gets worse.

Imagine a friend who comes to you with has a massive debt with an astronomical interest rate. This friend has a lovely family with young children, but soon they may not have anywhere to live because the creditors are attempting to take their home. Deeply concerned, you ask this friend how paying off the debt is coming along. Nonchalantly they reply, "Oh . . . I don't know . . . I think I'm going to give it some time. It's really not *that* bad." Of course, you know the truth of the matter. If you're a true friend, you'll bypass the social niceties and plead with this person (Proverbs 27:6). You know that debt like this will destroy your friend's life and cripple their family for years to come.

Sin is far graver because it eats away at our souls. The debt of unconfessed sin grows until it consumes you and everything you hold precious. Yet it isn't uncommon for us to hear—or to say—"it's not *that* bad." Don't for a minute buy into the lie that if you try to ignore or deny your sins, they will simply go away. If someone said "no big deal" about their loans and stopped paying on them, they'd be headed for financial crisis. How much more diligent should we be when dealing with our sin, which seeks to bankrupt our souls? The Puritan John Owen said,

> He that stands still and suffers his enemies to double
> blows upon him without resistance, will undoubtedly
> be conquered in the issue. If sin be subtle, watchful,
> strong, and always at work in the business of kill-
> ing our souls, and we be slothful, negligent, foolish,
> in proceeding to the ruin thereof, can we expect a
> comfortable event? There is not a day but sin foils or
> is foiled, prevails or is prevailed on; and it will be so
> whilst we live in this world.[6]

Let me be your friend for a moment. If you are hoping secret sins will get better with time, you're deceived. Uncon- fessed sin will only continue to gather interest and grow. Ignoring it will lead to spiritual crisis as the sins you thought you could manage one day reveal themselves to be crushing weights (Psalms 38:4; 40:12; Hebrews 12:1). Maybe you feel crushed by sins that have gotten out of hand in your life right now. There's hope.

Only God can forgive your debt

In September of 2019, Union Theological Seminary had a unique chapel service that received nationwide attention. The seminary tweeted, "Today in chapel, we confessed to plants. Together we held our grief, joy, regret, hope, guilt and sorrow in prayer; offering them to the beings who sustain us but whose gifts we too often fail to honor. What do you confess to the plants in your life?"[7] A picture of several students sitting around various houseplants accompanied the tweet that sounded like a parody piece written by the Babylon Bee.[8]

In confession, we recognize that God is the ultimate offended party when we sin (Psalm 51:4). Because this is true, only God has the right to pardon our debts. This is a crucial point in our therapeutic society. At a time when many are tempted to believe that the only forgiveness they need is their own, the Scriptures provide us with a healthy corrective. Dietrich Bonhoeffer addressed this in his classic work on Christian community, *Life Together*. He wrote the following:

> Why is it that it is often easier for us to confess our
> sins to God than to a brother? . . . [If this is the case]
> we must ask ourselves whether we have not often been
> deceiving ourselves with our confession of sin to God,
> whether we have not rather been confessing our sins
> to ourselves and also granting ourselves absolution.
> . . . Self-forgiveness can never lead to a breach with
> sin; this can be accomplished only by the judging and
> pardoning Word of God itself.[9]

Bonhoeffer's point is that sometimes, instead of truly confessing our sins, we simply give lip service to the Lord without a genuine intention of parting ways with the things that cause our debt to mount. Instead of looking to Christ, we look to appease our troubled consciences through a counterfeit forgiveness. You can't grant yourself absolution any more than a houseplant can! Only God can remove the debts we carry, which is why Jesus taught us to pray to the Father, "Forgive us our debts." While you can receive forgiveness directly from God through Jesus Christ, Bonhoeffer was correct in stating that confession to a Christian brother or sister (or trusted church leader) can be a helpful tool for bringing your debts into the light. When they're out in the open, you can't minimize them any longer; and it's when we confess them truly that we experience the radical forgiveness of God in Christ.

What about Forgiving Others?

To the petition "Forgive us our debts," Jesus added, "as we also have forgiven our debtors" (Matthew 6:12). He further expanded on this in verses 14–15, "For if you forgive others their trespasses, your heavenly Father will also forgive you, but if you do not forgive others their trespasses, neither will your Father forgive your trespasses."

C. S. Lewis observed that "Everyone thinks forgiveness is a lovely idea until they have something to forgive."[10] According to a recent Barna study, nearly one in four practicing Christians has someone in their life they cannot forgive.[11] While the biblical principle of *lex talionis*—an eye for an eye and a tooth for a tooth—comes naturally to us, forgiveness does not. An unforgiving heart is very different from the heart of Jesus though. So much so that Jesus here seems to correlate God forgiving us with our forgiving other people.

In his book *Forgive*, Tim Keller says forgiveness is a "form of voluntary suffering" because in forgiveness we bear the cost of the offense rather than seek revenge.

> Forgiveness means that, when you want to make them suffer, instead you refuse to do it. And this refusal

is *hard*. It is difficult and costly, but through it you
are absorbing the debt yourself. Some think that by
remaining angry they are giving the wrongdoers what
they deserve. But in reality you are enabling their
actions to continue to hurt you.[12]

What if the person who has sinned against you hasn't
repented—must you still extend forgiveness to them? Here
it's helpful to distinguish between forgiveness, reconciliation,
and restoration. Based on Jesus's teaching in the Lord's Prayer,
we are called to forgive everyone whether they repent or not.
This is important because if we're waiting on what someone
else does to determine whether we forgive them, bitterness and
hatred will begin to brew in our hearts. We can get stuck in
this bondage while we wait for someone else to come around to
see the pain they've caused us. Instead, we're called to forgive,
and this looks like laying aside our hatred and the desire for
harm to befall the person in question. Pray for their good, and
if they aren't believers, for their salvation (Matthew 5:44).

This doesn't mean overlooking the offense or not seeking
justice. If a husband abuses his wife, she can truly forgive him
while still calling the police and bringing the matter before
the church for discipline. In cases of abuse, this would actually
be the loving thing to do! True forgiveness does not need to
downplay the ways we've been sinned against in order for it to
be offered. It doesn't pretend all is okay when sin continues to
destroy, and it loves by holding the offender accountable while
also longing for their repentance.

You can forgive from the heart even if the other person
doesn't repent, but reconciliation *depends* on repentance. In
reconciliation, the person recognizes their sin and confesses
it. God calls us to pursue reconciliation in our relationships,
especially within the body of Christ. Too often we are content to "forgive and forget" while still harboring sinful attitudes

toward a brother or sister in Christ. In reconciliation, we recognize and confess our sins and embrace the healing that comes through Jesus. We're no longer at enmity with each other, and both parties have admitted the hurt they have caused, bringing a sense of peace to the relationship (Matthew 5:24).

Restoration is the next step in the process, and it goes further than reconciliation in that it restores the relationship that previously existed. You can be reconciled to someone truly, but sometimes it takes a long time to rebuild trust and restore what had been there previously. We shouldn't assume that once we're reconciled to someone, everything is going to immediately be as it was before. Furthermore, in some circumstances, restoration could be unwise. You're obligated to forgive, and God calls you to seek reconciliation, but you are not always called to restore.

A person who embezzles money might be forgiven, and they might reconcile with the people they have hurt along the way, but it would be foolish to hastily restore them to a position that would tempt them to do it again. Or consider the example of a pastor who has fallen into some grievous sin. There can be genuine forgiveness and even reconciliation between the pastor and those he has affected, but *restoration* to the ministry (especially if done prematurely) would be unwise and harmful. Jesus always calls us to forgive, and we should pursue reconciliation with others—seeking to live peaceably, while prayerfully considering the implications of restoration.

Is God's Forgiveness of Me Dependent on My Forgiveness of Others?

At first glance, it does seem as though this is what Jesus is teaching here, doesn't it? If you don't forgive, then how can you expect God to forgive you?

Our forgiveness of others should flow out of the forgiveness we've received from God. Consider again the parable of the unforgiving servant. The king forgave an insurmountable debt, but the forgiven servant went on to punish one of his fellow servants who owed him a trivial amount. The point of the parable is to highlight how tragic it is when we who have been forgiven so much withhold mercy from our debtors. Forgiveness is an obligation of the forgiven, not something earned by forgiving.

If sin is a debt that is growing, crushing, and enslaving, there's no payment we can offer to God for our pardon. Considering the immensity of our sin, it's hard to imagine a situation in which we could pray, "Father, I forgave this person; therefore, you owe me forgiveness."

Jesus is here making an argument from lesser to greater. This is meant to give us confidence that God will indeed forgive us when we pray to him. As Herman Witsius says, it's as if we were saying to God, "O Lord, we, whose kindness is always narrow and scanty, are influenced by such affections toward our neighbor as to forgive him cordially his offenses against us. With how much greater boldness may we ask such a favor from thee, whose vast kindness knows neither bounds nor limits."[13]

When Jesus taught us to pray for forgiveness, he highlighted both the serious nature of our sin and the generous forgiveness of our God. He's the only one who never needed to pray for the forgiveness of his debts, but he prayed and provided for the forgiveness of our debts. As the perfectly righteous one, he allowed himself to be crushed by our debts so that we might be loosed from them (Isaiah 53:5–6). On the cross he cried out, *Tetelestai!* which means to finish, fulfill, or *pay what is due* (John 19:30).[14] You can boldly pray for the forgiveness of your debts not because you're sinless, but because the sinless one cried out, "Paid in full!" The apostle Paul reminded the Colossians, "And you, who were dead in your trespasses and the uncircumcision of your flesh, God made alive together with him, having forgiven us all our trespasses, *by canceling the record of debt that stood against us* with its legal demands. This he set aside, nailing it to the cross" (Colossians 2:13–14). If you feel crushed right now, lift your eyes to the One who was crushed in your place, and hear his voice speaking from heaven, saying, "I have paid what you owed; your debts are canceled!"

A Prayer from the Past

O Lord, if your wisdom, holiness, and goodness command me to taste the bitterness of my sins; if I must want for a time the greatly desired light of your countenance, for the sake of which I would cheerfully part with every thing that is most delightful in this world; If I must experience the bitterness of your indignation, which is more distressing to me than death itself, and which, I know that I have deserved; yet, O Lord, I do not withdraw, and have no right to withdraw myself from your authority. Here I am ready to endure without a murmur whatever it shall be your good pleasure to lay upon me. Only lay not on me your wrath and curse; chasten me in moderation, for my correction, not for destruction; and when I will have been chastened, receive me at length into your friendship, lay aside the rod, let the light of your countenance cheer me; "make me to hear joy and gladness, that the bones which you have broken may rejoice."

—HERMAN WITSIUS[15]

Prayer Practices

1. Think of one person who has hurt you that you struggle to forgive. Commit to praying for them this week, asking God to soften your heart toward them, while also praying for their genuine repentance. Talk to a friend you trust about this process.
2. Read Psalms 38 and 51. Spend some time this week praying through them and making the words of the

psalmist your own. Where the psalmist confesses his sins specifically, think about specific things in your life you need to experience God's forgiveness for, and pray with those in mind.

Questions for Discussion

1. What benefits are there of having someone in your life that you can be honest with about sin? Do you currently have this type of relationship?
2. Where do you struggle with the differences between forgiveness, reconciliation, and restoration? What barriers to each of these have you experienced in your own life?
3. What does it say about us if we have an unforgiving heart? Where would you encourage someone to look who was struggling to forgive someone?

Chapter Ten

Lead Us Not into Temptation

We see then that, notwithstanding all our gifts and how great they might be, we are nothing without God's help. When he leaves us alone to our own devices, our own knowledge and wisdom are worthless. Unless he sustains us, not even the highest educational degree, no not even theology itself, is worth anything to us, for in the hour of temptation, it so happens that the devil with his snares shuts our eyes to the Scriptures that comfort us. . . . Let us learn that if God withdrew his hand we would be defeated. Let no one glory in his own righteousness, wisdom, or other gifts. With humility let us pray with the apostles, "Lord, increase our faith" (Luke 17:5).

—Martin Luther, sixteenth-century
German theologian and reformer

In the final petition of the Lord's Prayer, Jesus teaches us to ask for divine protection against temptation and Satan. The first part of this petition stands alone as a request for God not to do something—*don't* lead us into temptation!

Do Jesus's words suggest that God puts us in compromising situations? In 2019, Pope Francis approved changes to the wording of the Lord's Prayer in Roman Catholic liturgy from "Lead us not into temptation" to "Do not let us fall into temptation." He reasoned that the traditional language made God out to be the bad guy. This change would better convey the truth that God doesn't push us into sin, but instead—like any good father—is waiting to pick us up when we fall.

So, which is it? Does God lead us into temptation, or do we wander there on our own?

Temptation Defined and Defeated

It's worth noting that the word *temptation* has a broad semantic range in the New Testament. This means that the word can have a different sense depending on the context it's used in. You're familiar with this in the English language. If I say to you, "That pizza was the bomb!" you know that the word *bomb* doesn't mean the same thing as if I used it in the context of military combat. Context is the greatest factor when it comes to determining a word's meaning. In some places, the word Jesus used in Matthew 6:13 refers to *testing*, as in undergoing thorough examination. Paul said in 2 Corinthians 13:5, "Examine [test] yourselves, to see whether you are in the faith." Of course, Paul wasn't encouraging the Corinthians to open themselves up to sinful temptation!

In other contexts, the word is used when someone is trying to set a trap for another person. Satan tempted Jesus in the wilderness (Mark 1:13; Luke 4:12), trying to induce him to commit idolatry. Here the word means to *sinfully entice*. While the wicked in Scripture do this (Psalms 57:6; 141:9), God doesn't. James said, "Let no one say when he is tempted, 'I am being tempted by God,' for God cannot be tempted with evil, and he himself tempts no one" (James 1:13). God never forces you to sin. He isn't cruelly putting you in hopeless situations to make you fall. When it comes to evil, no one can ever say to God, "You made me do it!"

On the other hand, this petition reminds us that God is sovereign over the avenues of temptation. To pray *lead us not into temptation, but deliver us from evil* is to recognize God's power over the sinister forces that seek to undermine our faith in Jesus Christ, and to depend on his grace to overcome those forces. While we do well to never imply that God is the author of evil (something universally rejected by Christians), the traditional rendering of Matthew 6:13 faithfully communicates the truth that while God doesn't *make* us sin, he's able to keep us from temptation and sin.

Herman Witsius in his study on the Lord's Prayer noted how this petition expresses "very emphatically the powerful, but just, holy, and pure providence of God regarding tempters, temptation, and the consequence of temptation."[1] He highlighted three ways God is sovereign over temptation:

1. God alone gives the tempter permission to act. As one example, Witsius appealed to Ahab's deception in 1 Kings 22:22, but the story of Job also makes this clear (Job 1:6–12).
2. Sometimes God's providence places us in the presence of temptation. Here we might consider Jesus being led into the wilderness by the Spirit where Satan would confront him (Matthew 4:1).
3. Witsius noted that God sometimes withholds the heavenly assistance that enables us to better resist temptation. As an example, he gave 2 Chronicles 32:21, where God left King Hezekiah to himself that he might test him.[2]

So while God doesn't make us sin, he's our only hope against sinning. In this petition, we ask God to shackle Satan's influence in our lives, to protect us from those situations that draw us away from the Lord, and to give us the divine assistance we need to act courageously in the day of temptation.

Three Sources of Sinful Temptation

The Puritan John Owen wrote what may be the most comprehensive treatment of sin and temptation. There he defined *temptation* as anything that "causes or occasions [a man] to sin, or in anything to go off from his duty, either by bringing evil into his heart, or drawing out that evil that is in his heart, or any other way diverting him from communion with God . . ."[3] Among tempters that seek to bring evil into our hearts from without, the devil and ungodly influences are the most common culprits in Scripture.

The devil

Jesus talked about the devil in the second half of this petition. *Deliver us from evil* is probably a reference to the tempter himself. The word *evil* is used later in Matthew with reference to Satan (Matthew 13:19, cf. John 17:15). And in the context of spiritual warfare Paul wrote that we're to raise the shield of faith so that we might "extinguish all the flaming darts of the evil one" (Ephesians 6:16). Satan was often referred to as the evil one by Jesus and the apostles, suggesting he's in view in the latter part of this petition.

This means that we can't honestly pray this petition and be oblivious to Satan's influences. The stakes are too high for you to be blind to the spiritual battle happening all around you. Of course, we can over-spiritualize every bad thing that happens to us and attribute it to demonic attack. Perhaps you've heard the following joke: How many Christians does it take to change a lightbulb? Ten! One to change the lightbulb and nine to pray against the spirit of darkness.

We shouldn't suppose that Satan is lurking beneath every sinus infection or parley with sin. At the same time, we shouldn't assume that the forces of evil are on vacation. To pray for daily deliverance is to recognize that Satan and his forces are daily seeking to ensnare us, a reality I suspect we're mostly unmindful of. The Lord's Prayer doesn't permit us to continue insensibly.

In the preface to his book *The Screwtape Letters*, C. S. Lewis said he believed we fall into two equal and opposite errors regarding Satan. He called these the errors of the materialist and the magician. The error of the materialist is to live like Satan doesn't exist. The error of the magician is to have an excessive and unhealthy interest in the forces of evil.[4] This petition helps us to understand that we can't dismiss Satan, like the materialist, but that we also shouldn't give him too much credit, like the magician. God has dealt the evil one a mortal wound through the cross of Jesus Christ, and he breaks the spell of Satan everywhere that the gospel is proclaimed.

Ungodly influences

Ungodly influences, sometimes simply referred to as "sinners" in the Bible, are another source of temptation for the believer (Psalm 1:1, 5). Consider just a few verses:

- "Let not your heart envy sinners, but continue in the fear of the LORD all the day" (Proverbs 23:17).
- "Be not envious of evil men, nor desire to be with them" (Proverbs 24:1).
- "Do not be deceived: 'Bad company ruins good morals'" (1 Corinthians 15:33).

St. Augustine told the story of his friend Alypius, who after having been influenced by Augustine to part ways with the sinful celebrations of the pagan world, found himself again entangled in them when traveling to Rome as a student. At the time, Rome hosted the deadly gladiatorial games in the amphitheater, a sport known for its carnal brutality.

One evening after dinner, a group of Alypius's classmates began to entice him to join them for the spectacle. At first, he was resolute, "If you drag my body to that place and sit me down there, do not imagine you can turn my mind and my eyes to those spectacles. I shall be as one not there, and so I shall overcome both you and the games."[5] His peers didn't back down. Imploring even more, they tested his fortitude until he at last consented.

The group took their seats, eager to witness the barbarism, but Alypius clenched his eyes shut. That was until he heard the first roar of the audience in response to some fatal blow. Overcome with an unholy curiosity and self-dependence, Augustine writes that when Alypius opened his eyes, "He was struck in the soul by a wound graver than the gladiator in his body, whose fall had caused the roar. The shouting entered by his ears and forced open his eyes. Thereby it was the means of wounding and striking to the ground a mind still more bold than strong, and the weaker for the reason that he presumed on himself when he ought to have relied on [God]."[6]

Peer pressure got the better of poor Alypius, who wouldn't become a follower of Christ until later in his life. It also gets the better of Christians. The apostle Peter used to enjoy fellowship with non-Jewish believers in Jesus until certain Jewish believers from Jerusalem showed up. Fearing what these Jews might think, Peter started avoiding the very people he had once enjoyed meals with! Things got so bad that Paul had to confront Peter's peer-induced hypocrisy (Galatians 2:11–14). If it could happen to an apostle, it can happen to you.

Like Alypius, we tell ourselves we're capable of handling certain pressures and temptations. We never just say, "I'm going to give in to sin!" Instead we wander as closely to the fire as we can and imagine that while there, we'll just keep our eyes closed. We don't recognize that the chains that carry us toward sin are constructed from the same self-confidence that convinces us we're above temptation.

Our own hearts

On top of the external forces that may seek to entice us, we also must fight against our own unbridled desires. James said, "But each person is tempted when he is lured and enticed by his own desire" (James 1:14). This internal struggle is the most discouraging for many Christians. If it wasn't enough that Satan and sinners want to see us stumble, pile on the fact that sometimes—without their enticements—we run willingly into the arms of temptation. As much as we'd like to blame external forces for our sinning, often it's our own desires that lure us into the pit of iniquity.

John Owen's illustration helps us to consider the traitor within: "If a castle or fort be never so strong and well fortified, yet if there be a treacherous party within, that is ready to betray it on every opportunity, there is no preserving it from the enemy. There are traitors in our hearts, ready to take part, to close and side with every temptation, and to give up all to them . . ."[7] Proverbs 28:26 says, "Whoever trusts in his own mind is a fool, but he who walks in wisdom will be delivered." The Hebrew word for mind, *leyv*, is most often rendered *heart*, referring at times to the physical organ of the body, but often to one's inner self, the seat of feeling and emotions.[8]

No matter how well fortified our walls are against external foes, if we're not conscious of the enemy within, we're vulnerable to temptation. In a world that often says, "Follow your heart," wisdom says, "Don't always trust it!"

Three Strategies for Vigilance Against Temptation

The importance of this petition should be readily apparent. We are engaged in conflict with a stealthy enemy, outnumbered by a world system that loves to see Christians fall, and often betrayed by our own hearts, which are prone to making peace treaties with the very sin that would do us in. We are hopeless apart from the heavenly assistance that Jesus taught us to ask for each day. In addition to praying, we must also be vigilant, doing everything we can to guard against temptation. Jesus said, "*Watch and pray* that you may not enter into temptation. The spirit indeed is willing, but the flesh is weak" (Matthew 26:41, emphasis added). We will consider the following ways we can be proactive as we pray against temptation.

1. Keep your eyes in the right place

In the Bible, temptation often starts with the eye. In the early chapters of Genesis, when Eve was deceived by the serpent, she saw with her eyes that the forbidden tree was desirable for food (Genesis 3:6). King David, while taking a stroll on his palace roof, ogled at Bathsheba before he forcibly took her (2 Samuel 11:2). In his attempt to entice Jesus, Satan gave him a vision of the world's kingdoms and offered them to him in exchange for worship (Matthew 4:8). Praying watchfully means being aware of the temptations we're susceptible to and asking God to transform our desires. A watchful eye involves more than the ocular orbs in our head. In Scripture what we set our eyes upon has to do with what we longingly pursue. We are to "look" to Jesus (Hebrews 12:2), instead of setting our hearts upon the sin that so easily entangles us.

The story of Joseph in Scripture helps to illustrate what I mean. While Joseph was in Potiphar's house, Potiphar's wife "cast her eyes" on the handsome Joseph and tried to seduce him (Genesis 39:6–7). As tempting as the situation must have been, Joseph's eyes were focused on something else. He said to her, "Behold, because of me my master has no concern about anything in the house, and he has put everything that he has in my charge. He is not greater in this house than I am, nor has he kept back anything from me except you, because you are his wife. How then can I do this great wickedness and sin against God?" (vv. 8–9). Potiphar's wife has her gaze set on Joseph, but Joseph's gaze is set on the grace that God had shown him. He recounted the blessings of God: charge over Potiphar's entire household and innumerable privileges that accompanied his role. Focusing on God's kindness was a barrier of protection for him in the hour of temptation.

In his treatise on the mortification of sin in believers, John Owen encouraged Christians fighting with temptation to "bring their lust to the gospel."[9] The moment you feel the warmth of temptation's fire, fix your eyes on the great mercy God has shown you in Christ. Gaze at the cross, where the tempter was defeated and your forgiveness was purchased. Joseph, in the moment of temptation, meditated on the temporal blessings God had given him to resist lustful enticements. In the treasury of our blessings, we have the everlasting love of the Father, the precious blood of the Son, and the marvelous grace of the Spirit. When by faith we perceive these blessings, the fires of lust begin to dampen.

There's an old legend about the Protestant Reformer Martin Luther. As it goes, when Luther felt Satan tempting him, he would shout out "I am baptized!" Some sources even say he would write the phrase on the desk in his study so that he would never lose sight of the promises of God made to him in his baptism. When temptation comes, grab it by the neck and drag it into the light of God's goodness in the gospel, saying with Joseph, "How then can I do this great wickedness and sin against God?" As our eyes are firmly fixed on God's gracious promises to us in the gospel, they're less prone to wander.

2. Be quick to retreat

The second strategy for avoiding temptation is also clear from the story of Joseph. When Potiphar's wife finally got a hold of him, he fled the scene with such haste that he left some of his clothes behind (Genesis 39:11–18)! Retreating isn't usually considered a strategy for victory, but in the case of the fight against temptation, the Bible says it is. Think of the repeated exhortations given by the apostle Paul:

- "Flee from sexual immorality" (1 Corinthians 6:18).
- "Flee youthful passions and pursue righteousness, faith, love, and peace, along with those who call on the Lord from a pure heart" (2 Timothy 2:22).
- "No temptation has overtaken you that is not common to man. God is faithful, and he will not let you be tempted beyond your ability, but with the temptation he will also provide the way of escape, that you may be able to endure it" (1 Corinthians 10:13).

God doesn't tempt his children; instead, he gives us "exits," escape routes that he calls us to dart toward in the heat of battle. It might be the phone call you get from a family member the moment you're about to make a bad decision, a Scripture that comes to your mind, or a friend who instead of drawing gossip out of you doesn't indulge you in it. God will open the door for you to escape, and when he does, he says "run!" Once you've fled, give no provision to the enemy.

3. Adopt a scorched-earth policy

During WWII, the scorched-earth policy was one of the most brutal military strategies used against the invading German army. As Russian forces retreated, they "scorched the earth" behind them, destroying everything that could be valuable to the incoming army: food and water sources, buildings, communication centers, transportation, etc. The idea was to remove anything that might be a provision for the enemy. If it could serve as a foothold from whence the Germans might regain strength or muster an attack, it was to be destroyed.

These are the kinds of drastic measures we should take against sinful temptation. Jesus said "If your right eye causes you to sin, tear it out and throw it away. For it is better that you lose one of your members than that your whole body be thrown into hell" (Matthew 5:29). Paul wrote, "But put on the Lord Jesus Christ, and make no provision for the flesh, to gratify its desires" (Romans 13:14). When you know that something is an occasion for you to sin, don't give it resources to continue as a base of operations against your soul. When temptation comes knocking at the door, it is never wise to open it for negotiation. In fact, the house at which it comes to knock is often better left scorched.

What does a scorched-earth policy against temptation look like practically? It's different for each person, depending on what kinds of enticements allure us. Ask yourself, *what temptation am I most susceptible to?* Then consider potential lifelines that continue to feed that temptation's strength in your life. For example, the person struggling with pornography may find phone apps or internet websites that are better left scorched than searched. If you're drawn to gossip, scorching the earth might look like avoiding certain conversations or confessing the struggle to others who can hold you accountable. The person tempted to sloth may discover that the lifeline to their laziness is an unhealthy relationship with food or alcohol. We can keep from being lured into temptation as we do the hard work of identifying personal stumbling blocks and avoiding them.

Hope for the Tempted

I mentioned the scene in Galatians 2 where Paul had to confront Peter earlier in this chapter. Peter's cowardice and fear of man got the better of him, and his behavior sent the wrong message to his Gentile family in Christ. By not eating with them out of fear of the Jews, he was indicating that though they had believed in Jesus, they still weren't really a part of the family of God. What's striking about this encounter is that it was the very same sin—cowardice—that overcame Peter years prior on the night that he denied Jesus. Afraid of how others would treat him for following Jesus, Peter began to invoke a curse on himself, swearing, "I do not know the man" (Matthew 26:74).

Fast-forward many years later, after Jesus restored Peter over breakfast on the beach (John 21:15–19) and filled Peter with the gift of the Holy Spirit, leading him to preach a powerful sermon on the day of Pentecost (Acts 2:14). Despite Peter walking with Jesus, seeing his death and resurrection, and being filled with the Holy Spirit, *he still struggled with a temptation to cowardice.* If there was hope for Peter, even though he wrestled with the same sins throughout his life, then there's hope for you. Related to this, if Peter still had to fight every day to put to death those old passions that waged war against his soul, you will too. This is why we pray that God would lead us not into temptation but deliver us from evil. Just like Jesus delivered Peter, he will rescue all his sons and daughters from the mouth of the lion, Satan.

Recall again the words of Christ to Peter, "Satan demanded to have you, that he might sift you like wheat, *but I have prayed for you that your faith may not fail*" (Luke 22:31–32). Even when we do fall, Jesus doesn't give up on us. He remains and ever will be in our corner, our advocate before the heavenly Father (1 John 2:1–2). Additionally, his incarnation made him perfectly fit to sympathize with you amid temptation: "He had to be made like his brothers in every respect, so that he might become a merciful and faithful high priest in the service of God, to make propitiation for the sins of the people. For because he himself has suffered when tempted, he is able to help those who are being tempted" (Hebrews 2:17–18).

God doesn't forsake the tempted—even when we focus our eyes on the wrong things, run toward temptation instead

of fleeing it, and water the ground where sin grows instead
of scorching the earth. But don't be deceived: embracing our
tempters will attract the loving discipline of God. It's a grievous
thing to dabble in darkness after we've been rescued from its
dominion (Colossians 1:13), and we can't do so without experiencing the consequences. However, struggling sinners grieved
by their sin need not fear the condemnation of God. On the
cross, Jesus, like a magnet, pulled all our sins onto himself
and fully exhausted the holy justice of God in his own body.
He overcame temptation and Satan throughout his life, and
in his sinless victory we have salvation. Let us then take every
precaution to guard and cultivate the gifts God has generously
bestowed upon us, keeping watch with a sober mind as we pray
lead us not into temptation, but deliver us from evil.

A Prayer from the Past

*O dear Lord God, Father, this life of ours is so wretched,
so full of sorrow and misfortune, so full of danger and
insecurity, so full of evil and faithlessness—as St. Paul
says, 'The days are evil' (Ephesians 5:16)—that we might
justifiably be tired of life and even desirous of death. But
you, dear Father, know our weakness. Therefore, help us
to survive such great evil and malice. And when our time
comes, let it be a blessed hour and a joyful departure out
of this place of sorrows, that we may neither fear death
nor give way to despair, but in unwavering faith commit
our souls into your hands. Amen.*

—Martin Luther

Prayer Practices

1. What do you consider the lifelines to your personal sin
   struggles? Spend time praying that God would 1) reveal
   them to you, and 2) help you to wisely discern how to
   "scorch the earth."

2. Read 1 Thessalonians 4:3 and 1 John 5:14–15. Sometimes in the fight against temptation we can feel alone. What do these verses teach us about the confidence we can have when praying *Lead us not into temptation?*

Questions for Discussion

1. Discuss God's sovereignty over temptation. Can you think of any biblical examples where God kept an individual from sinning?
2. Alypius was drawn to the brutality of the gladiatorial games. Thinking about his story, where did he go wrong? Do you that you need to be more vigilant against things that allure you?
3. Discuss the three strategies for vigilance. Are there any additional strategies rooted in scriptural principles that have proven helpful in your own life?

Conclusion

The Sweet Smell of Prayer

We worship the Fashioner of the universe, declaring him, as we have been taught, to have no need of blood and libations and incense, but praising him by the word of prayer and thanksgiving for all that he has given us. We have learned that the only honor worthy of him is, not to consume by fire the things he has made for our nourishment, but to devote them to our use and those in need, in thankfulness to him sending up solemn prayers and hymns for our creation and all the means of health, for the variety of creatures and the changes of the seasons, and sending up our petitions that we may live again in incorruption through our faith in him. It is Jesus Christ who has taught us these things.

—Justin Martyr, second-century
Christian apologist

Exodus shows a scene where Moses argues with God because he feels unfit to be Yahweh's spokesman (Exodus 4). God told him to go and preach to Pharaoh, and Moses contended that he wasn't a very good public speaker. Fortunately, we're not all called to teach like Moses was, but we are all called to pray. I hope that this book has equipped you to mount the

Lord's Prayer and ride off with it—getting lost in communion with God as you take the scenic route through each petition. But the fact is, like Moses, our words are still ineloquently feeble (Exodus 4:10). Try as we may to be disciplined and believe that the transcendently intimate One is attentive to our cries, we're often drowsy and still have our doubts. It's not uncommon for the praying man or woman to feel like a failure. Why would God want to listen to *me*?

The truth is that God doesn't just hear your prayers; he *delights* in them! I want you to know that through Jesus, your prayers are the pleasant aroma that fills God's temple. Throughout Scripture, one of the symbols used to represent prayer is incense. Psalm 141:2 says, "Let my prayer be counted as incense before you, and the lifting up of my hands as the evening sacrifice!" In his vision of heaven's worship, John saw celestial beings holding harps "and golden bowls full of incense, which are the prayers of the saints" (Revelation 5:8).

Later in Revelation, the prayers of God's people are offered *with* much incense "and the smoke of the incense, with the prayers of the saints, rose before God from the hand of the angel" (Revelation 8:4). Through Christ, God sweetens our prayers, making them an aroma pleasing to him.

The fragrant incense that filled the Jerusalem temple in the Old Testament helped to cover the smell of sacrificial blood and carcasses (constant reminders of sin and the need for forgiveness), and the rising smoke depicted the prayers of God's people ascending to him. We don't have a temple or altar of incense today because the prayers of God's people—our prayers—are the fulfillment of those ancient rites. God spoke through the prophet Malachi about the incense offered: "For from the rising of the sun to its setting my name will be great among the nations, and in every place incense will be offered to my name, and a pure offering. For my name will be great among the nations, says the LORD of hosts" (Malachi 1:11).

Now the smoke doesn't just rise from Jerusalem, but from every place on earth, including your prayer closet. Our prayers are the perfume of heaven, which are made fragrant in Jesus.

The sacrificial imagery associated with incense in the Bible also reminds us that prayer is costly. It's okay if building the habit of prayer that I've spoken of in this book doesn't come easily to you. In fact, you shouldn't expect it to. *It's a sacrifice.* Cultivating a strong prayer life will require putting time on the altar, and those busy with pursuits, whether they're worthy or worthless, find it hard to offer up even five minutes. Let me suggest that you seek to give to God your *best* time in prayer. Just like the Israelites were called to offer the unblemished animals, don't give God the leftovers. Wherever you find them, give God your best moments in prayer because the sacrifice of prayer is always worth it.

Your prayers result in God's action on earth. In Revelation 8 after the incense-mingled prayers reached God's nostrils, John records that "the angel took the censer and filled it with fire from the altar and threw it on the earth, and there were peals of thunder, rumblings, flashes of lightning, and an earthquake" (Revelation 8:5). In effect, John sees how the prayers of God's people were instrumental in God executing justice among the nations. Prayer also mobilizes heaven. In Daniel 9, Daniel prays a prayer of repentance on behalf of God's people during the evening hour of prayer. While praying, the angel Gabriel came to him saying, "O Daniel, I have now come out to give you insight and understanding. At the beginning of your pleas for mercy a word went out, and I have come to tell it to you, for you are greatly loved" (Daniel 9:22–23). The moment Daniel started to plead for mercy, God sent an angel on a mission. Would you pray more if you knew that doing so moved not only the hearts of men, but the angels—even heaven? The costly sacrifice of prayer is a sweet-smelling aroma that God uses to transform the world.

Prayer doesn't just change the world, it changes *you*. We cannot enter into true prayer without coming into contact with the God whose very presence transforms his people. Eugene Peterson wrote, "When we pray, we are using words that bring us into proximity with words that break cedars, shake the wilderness, make the oaks whirl, and strip the forests bare (Psalm 29:5–9)."[1] Praying with Jesus refashions us into the image of Jesus and will never leave us unchanged.

The sacrificial-incense imagery symbolizing prayer also connects prayer to the concept of worship. This is one reason the Lord's Prayer is frequently concluded with the doxology, "For thine is the kingdom, and the power, and the glory, forever. Amen." In the Bible, prayer is often ended with a statement of praise, or doxology (e.g., Psalm 72:19–20).[2] Many ancient Gospel manuscripts don't include the words of this doxology in Matthew 6, but it's clear from other passages of Scripture that the words themselves are thoroughly biblical (even if they aren't original to Matthew's Gospel).

The concluding doxology echoes Daniel's words to King Nebuchadnezzar of Babylon: "You, O king, the king of kings, to whom the God of heaven has given the kingdom, the power, and the might, and the glory" (Daniel 2:37). The doxology emphasizes the fact that God is the source of all blessing and authority. Similarly, King David prayed, "Blessed are you, O LORD, the God of Israel our father, forever and ever. Yours, O LORD, is the greatness and the power and the glory and the victory and the majesty, for all that is in the heavens and in the earth is yours. Yours is the kingdom, O LORD, and you are exalted as head above all" (1 Chronicles 29:10–11). These types of doxologies are also found in the New Testament (1 Timothy 1:17; Jude 25). True prayer *is* worship, and it always *leads* to more worship. It's the song of your heart to God, and your heart together with your whole body is called to make music. God help you to sing to the Father, in the Son, and by the grace of the Holy Spirit.

Endnotes

Introduction

1. Tertullian, Cyprian, & Origen, *On the Lord's Prayer* (Crestwood, NY: St. Vladimir's Seminary Press, 2004), 42.

2. Tertullian, 70.

3. Kenneth E. Bailey, *Jesus Through Middle Eastern Eyes: Cultural Studies in the Gospels* (Downers Grove, IL: InterVarsity Press, 2008), 91.

4. Martin Luther, "A Simple Way to Pray: for Master Peter the Barber," 1535, https://wmpl.org/filed/resources/public/Literature/ASimpleWay toPray.pdf.

5. St. Gregory of Nyssa, *The Lord's Prayer, The Beatitudes* (New York/Mahwah, NJ: Paulist Press, 1954), 19.

Chapter One

1. Elder Porphyrios, *Wounded by Love: The Life and the Wisdom of Saint Porphyrios* (Evia, Greece: Denise Harvey, 2005), 31–32.

2. G. K. Beale, *The New International Greek Testament Commentary: The Book of Revelation* (Grand Rapids: William B. Eerdmans Company, 1999), 451.

3. S. M. Baugh, *The Majesty on High: Introduction to the Kingdom of God in the New Testament* (CreateSpace Independent Publishing Platform, 2017), 98.

4. Alfred Edersheim, *The Life and Times of Jesus the Messiah*, Vol. 1 (London: Longmans, Green , and Co., 1907), 93–94.

5. Charles Spurgeon, "Sovereign Grace and Man's Responsibility," Sermon No. 207, given August 1, 1958, at the Music Hall, Royal Surrey Gardens, Newington, Surrey, London, England, https://www .blueletterbible.org/Comm/spurgeon_charles/sermons/0207.cfm.

Chapter Two

1. John W. Kleinig, *Wonderfully Made: A Protestant Theology of the Body* (Bellingham, WA: Lexham Press, 2021), 10.

2. Emphasis added by author; and hereafter when italics are used in a passage of Scripture.

3. St. John Chrysostom, *Commentary on the Psalm*, trans. Robert Charles Hill (Brookline, MA: Holy Cross Orthodox Press, 2007), 2:280, commentary on Psalm 141.

4. Herman Witsius, *Sacred Dissertations on the Lord's Prayer* (Grand Rapids: Reformation Heritage Books, 2012), 100.

5. Tertullian, Cyprian, & Origen, *On the Lord's Prayer* (Crestwood, NY: St. Vladimir's Seminary Press, 2004), 67.

Chapter Three

1. C. Clifton Black, *The Lord's Prayer* (Louisville: Westminster John Knox Press, 2018), 150–56. This book gives a summary of the various translations.

2. Paul F. Bradshaw, *Daily Prayer in the Early Church* (Eugene, OR: Wipf and Stock, 2008), see 1 and 12–15 for the various kinds of prayer that became normative in the Jewish synagogue.

3. Bradshaw, 23.

4. Craig Keener, *Acts, Volume II* (Grand Rapids: Baker Academic, 2012), 1044: "At some point during the Hellenistic period, the time of the near-dusk offering shifted toward the middle of the afternoon (as in Acts 3:1), perhaps to avoid the risk of running late."

5. See *Didache* or *Teaching of the Twelve Apostles*, trans. Charles H. Hoole, Early Christian Writings, 8.3, http://www.earlychristianwritings .com/text/didache-hoole.html.

6. Herman Witsius, *Sacred Dissertations on the Lord's Prayer* (Grand Rapids: Reformation Heritage Books, 2012), 120.

7. Quoted by Witsius; see also John Calvin, *Calvin's Commentaries, Volume XVIII* (Grand Rapids: Baker Books, 2009) 418 (comments on Acts 10:9).

8. C. S. Lewis, *How to Pray* (New York: HarperOne, 2018), 90.

9. Arthur Bennett, ed., *The Valley of Vision: A Collection of Puritan Prayers and Devotions* (Edinburgh: Banner of Truth Trust, 1975).

Chapter Four

1. Gerhard Friedrich, ed., *Theological Dictionary of the New Testament* (Grand Rapids: Eerdmans, 1964/1976), 5.872.

2. John Calvin, *Institutes of the Christian Religion*, trans. Ford Lewis Battles (Louisville: Westminster John Knox Press, 2006), vol. III.XX.1.

3. Eugene H. Peterson, *Working the Angles: The Shape of Pastoral Integrity* (Grand Rapids: Eerdmans: 1987), 46.

4. John Calvin, *Institutes*, vol. III.XX.5.

5. Martin Luther, *A Simple Way to Pray*, 2nd ed. (Milwaukee: Northwestern Publishing House, 2017), 12.

6. Victor Lee Austin, *Losing Susan* (Grand Rapids: Brazos Press 2016), 50–51.

7. Austin, 50–51.

Chapter Five

1. Thomas Aquinas, *Summa Theologica*, Pt. II-II Q.83 art. 2 (Notre Dame: Christian Classics, 1948).

2. John Calvin, *Institutes*, vol. III.XX.3.

3. Augustine, "On the Lord's Prayer in St. Matthew's Gospel 6:9," Sermon VI.5, https://biblehub.com/library/augustine/sermons_on_selected_lessons_of_the_new_testament/sermon_vi_on_the_lords.htm.

4. Herman Witsius, *Sacred Dissertations on the Lord's Prayer* (Grand Rapids: Reformation Heritage Books, 2012), 194ff.

5. Witsius, *Sacred Dissertations*, 194ff.

6. Maximus the Confessor, *Selected Writings* (New York: Paulist Press, 1985), 99–126.

7. St. Gregory of Nyssa, *The Lord's Prayer, The Beatitudes* (New York: Paulist Press, 1954), 36.

8. Witsius, *Sacred Dissertations*, 191.

Chapter Six

1. Tertullian, Origen, & Cyprian, *On the Lord's Prayer* (Crestwood, NY: St. Vladimir's Seminary Press, 2004), 74.

2. John Calvin, *Institutes*, vol. III.XX.42.

3. *Institutes*, III. XX. 42.

4. *Institutes*, III. XX. 42.

Chapter Seven

1. Alexander Schmemann, *Our Father* (New York: St. Vladimir's Seminary Press, 2002), 46.

2. Martin Luther *Luther's Works Volume 73* (Saint Louis, MO: Concordia Publishing House, 2020), 86. See Luther's first disputation against the Antinomians, argument 14.

3. Luther, 79, or argument 7.

4. John of Damascus, *The Fathers of the Church, Volume XXXVII* (Washington, DC: The Catholic University of America Press, 2012), 297.

Chapter Eight

1. Everett Ferguson, *Background of Early Christianity* (Grand Rapids: Eerdmans, 2003), 85.

2. See James M. Kittelson and Hans H. Wiersma, *Luther the Reformer* (Minneapolis: Fortress Press, 2016), 250.

3. John Calvin, *Institutes*, Vol. III.XX.44.

4. Brother Andrew, *God's Smuggler* (New York: New American Library, 1967), chapter 6.

5. Brother Andrew, *God's Smuggler*, chapter 6.

6. Augustine, *Enchiridion On Faith, Hope, and Love,* trans. Albert C. Outler, 30.115, http://www.saintsbooks.net/books/St.%20Augustine%20 -%20Enchiridion%20on%20Faith,%20Hope,%20and%20Love.pdf.

7. Thomas Aquinas *Summa Theologica*, II-II q.83 Art. 6 (Notre Dame: Christian Classics, 1948).

8. Jaroslav Pelikan, *The Emergence of the Catholic Tradition (100-600)* (Chicago: University of Chicago Press, 1971), 82.

9. Tertullian, Cyprian, & Origen, *On the Lord's Prayer* (Crestwood, NY: St. Vladimir's Seminary Press, 2004), 46.

Chapter Nine

1. Grant Suneson, "How Much Mortgage Debt Does Your State Have? Two States Are Far and Away Above the Rest," *USA Today*, June 27, 2019.

2. Kayla Galloway, "Here's How Much Student Loan Debt Californians Owe as Biden Hints at Forgiveness," *KNBC Los Angeles*, Last modified May 3, 2022, https://www.nbclosangeles.com/news/ california-news/student-loan-debt-california-biden/2882343/.

3. David Lightman, "Eight Million Californians Have Auto Loans, but More and More Struggle to Pay Them Off," *Yahoo!finance*, Last modified April 4, 2023, https://finance.yahoo.com/news/eight-million-californians-auto-loans-130000177.html.

4. Alexandria White, "Alaskans Carry the Highest Credit Card Balance—Here's the Average Credit Card Balance in Every State," *CNBC*, Last modified May 9, 2023, https://www.cnbc.com/select/ average-credit-card-balance-by-state/.

5. Lane Gillespie, "Average American Debt Statistics," ed. Tori Rubloff, *Bankrate*, Last modified January 13, 2023, https://www .bankrate.com/personal-finance/debt/average-american-debt/.

6. John Owen, *Overcoming Sin and Temptation*, Redesign (Wheaton, IL: Crossway, 2015), 52.

7. Union Seminary (@UnionSeminary), Twitter, September 17, 2019 at 9:43 a.m., https://twitter.com/UnionSeminary/status/11740 00941667880960.

8. The Babylon Bee is a Christian satire website that pokes fun at Christian culture, politics, and various topics.

9. Dietrich Bonhoeffer, *Life Together* (New York: HarperOne, 1954), 115–16.

10. C. S. Lewis, *Mere Christianity* (New York: Harper San Francisco, 2001), 115.

11. Barna Group, "1 in 4 Practicing Christians Struggles to Forgive Someone," *The Mercy Journey*, April 11, 2019, https://www.barna.com/research/forgiveness-christians/.

12. Timothy Keller, *Forgive: Why Should I and How Can I?* (New York: Viking, 2022), 9.

13. Herman Witsius, *Sacred Dissertations on the Lord's Prayer* (Grand Rapids: Reformation Heritage Books, 2012), 324.

14. William F. Arndt and F. Wilbur Gingrich, *A Greek-English Lexicon of the New Testament and Other Early Christian Literature*, 3rd ed. (Chicago: University of Chicago Press, 2000), 998.

15. Witsius, *Sacred Dissertations*, 338.

Chapter Ten

1. Herman Witsius, *Sacred Dissertations on the Lord's Prayer* (Grand Rapids: Reformation Heritage Books, 2012), 355–57.

2. Witsius, *Sacred Dissertations*, 355–57.

3. John Owen, *Overcoming Sin and Temptation*, Redesign (Wheaton, IL: Crossway, 2015), 156.

4. C. S. Lewis, *The Screwtape Letters* (New York: HarperCollins, 1996), ix.

5. St. Augustine, *The Confessions (Oxford World's Classics)* (New York: Oxford University Press, 1998), 100.

6. St. Augustine, *The Confessions*, 100.

7. Owen, *Overcoming Sin and Temptation*, 171.

8. Ludwig Koehler, Walter Baumgartner, M. E. J. Richardson, and J. J. Stamm, *The Hebrew and Aramaic Lexicon of the Old Testament*, CD-Rom Edition (Boston: Brill, 2000), 514.

9. Owen, *Overcoming Sin and Temptation*, 104.

Conclusion

1. Eugene H. Peterson, *Working the Angles: The Shape of Pastoral Integrity* (Grand Rapids: William B Eerdmans, 1987), 43.

2. The book of Psalms is divided into five different books, each of which ends with a statement of doxology.